THE HINDU SYSTEM
OF
RELIGIOUS SCIENCE AND ART

THE HINDU SYSTEM
OF
RELIGIOUS SCIENCE AND ART

KISHORI LAL SARKAR

With a Foreword by

Professor Makhan Jha, Ph.D., D. Litt.

Department of Anthropology
Ranchi University, Ranchi

GYAN

GYAN PUBLISHING HOUSE

NEW DELHI-110 002

The Hindu System of Religious Science and Art

Kishori Lal Sarkar

(Religion, Culture, Arts, Indology)

ISBN : 81-212-0499-2

Reprinted in 1995 in India by
Gyan Publishing House
5 Ansari Road
New Delhi 110 002

Originally published in 1910

Printed at Tarun Offset Press, Delhi-110 053

FOREWORD

The author, late Kishori Lal Sarkar, was a great indologist and practiced law at the Calcutta High Court, and wrote this valuable book "The Hindu System of Religious Science and Art," which was published as early as in 1910 from Calcutta. In those days religion was being interpreted by the philosophers or by the orthodox pandits in their own ways to suit their needs. But the publication of this book by K.L. Sarkar brought a revolution in the field of study of religion in India.

Sarkar was of opinion that the religion has an access both in the fields of science and arts. He suggested that "religious science" is somewhat familiar but does not show the expression "religious art". Nevertheless there are things comprehended in religion which may be called art, just as much as there are things in it which may be presented in the shape of science.

The words—science and art, are not used in a uniform way. Sometimes the word art is used in contrast with nature, whereas the term science is applied to the elaborations of laws of nature. Keeping this interpretation in mind Sarkar suggested that art is conceived as something which is human, but not natural but as a matter of fact the human is also natural. In this connection it may also be argued that while "science consists in knowing, art consists in doing". I may also add further that art also consists in feeling.

Generally speaking, the knowledge of the truths of the material world is called science while a realization of the truth of the consciousness of man is called art. In spite of these differences science and art are equally the two forms of human culture and as culture forms the central theme of anthropology, the interpretation of religion as a science and art falls within the greater ambit of the science of man.

II

The author has discussed the various interpretations of religious science and art in this book and has organised all the materials into nine chapters, besides a brief introduction.

In the first chapter he throws light on the outline of the subject and he has also used different sub-headings like science and art in religion; rationalism and emotionalism; the revelation of *Gyan* and *Bhakti* etc., in interpreting universal form of religion. In the second chapter the author talks about the salient features of Hinduism. Here again he also used different sub-headings like the scientific study of the Hindu religion; the truths of the Hindu religion, Hinduism and salvation etc. In this chapter he has drawn references from the *Vedant Dharshan, Sankhya, Nyay, the Bhagwad Geeta,* the Mahabharata etc. He further argues that the true salient features of Hinduism are the *Yoga Vidya* and the *Mantra* Vidya—the two blessed arts for stirring and elevating the human soul and identifying it with the supreme soul. In the *Vedanta Darshan Vidya* is used in the sense of the highest art, while the Gyan in the sense of highest knowledge. In this way drawing references from the different schools of Indian Philosophy, the author makes an attempt to make interpretations of Hinduism in this chapter.

In the third chapter, he distinguishes rationalism and emotionalism which reveal the deity. He says emotionalism consists of personal affections. In its purely and exhausted sphere, its very existence lies in the realisation of the supreme personality reigning in the universe. However, rationalism follows an impersonal eleminating process, in arriving at the existence of the supreme being. It eliminates the accidental, the changeable and the gross neglect until it gets at the permanent, the unchangeable and the spiritual soul of all beings and things. In this chapter also the author has used many sub-headings with a view to explain the rationalism and emotionalism with a view to reveal the supreme God.

In the fourth chapter the author has taken the help of various texts specially the *Karma Kand* of the Vedic literatures and he quotes heavily from those sacred texts.

In the fifth chapter the author has described the *Gyan* and the *Bhakti Marg* of the Brahminic period with special reference to the concept of *Avtarism*. The next chapter i.e. sixth is devoted to the interpretations of only one text, the *Srimad Bhagwad Geeta*. The author explains, the *Bhagwad Geeta* from different angles and reveals the different *margas* for achieving salvation as prescribed for the Hindus.

In the seventh chapter the author discusses the *Darshan Sashtra* with special reference to the *Nyay*, the *Vaisheshika Darshan*, the *Vedanta Darshan*, the *Sankhya Darshan*, the *Patanjali Darshan* etc.

In the eighth chapter he talks about the general features of the Puranas with special references to Vaishnavism and Shaiva-Saktism. He also talks about the forms of *Sadhana*. Lastly, he also throws light on *Sri Gouranga* of Naddea (Chaitannya Maha Prabhu).

In the last chapter i.e. ninth, the author throws light on some of the miscellaneous features such as the *Karma* or the *Prabdha*, the future state of man, a sacred names of the diety etc.

Thus, considered from the point of view of serious interpretations of religion, I find that Kishori Lal Sarkar made a praise worthy attempt to explain the Hindu religion, both as a science and art as early as in 1910 when religion was considered to be the subject matter of orthodox pandits and classical intelligentsia. I hope, the work of this great author is being reprinted by the Gyan Publishing House, New Delhi for wider circulation which will be well received by the students of religion in India and abroad.

Department of Anthropology, **MAKHAN JHA**
U.G.C., Centre of Advanced Study,
Ranchi University,
Ranchi.

CONTENTS

CHAPTER III.

DETAILED OBSERVATIONS AS TO HOW RATIONALISM AND EMOTIONALISM REVEAL THE DEITY.

CHAPTER IV.

ILLUSTRATIVE TEXTS OF THE TWO REVELATIONS FROM THE VEDAS.

CHAPTER V.

THE DOUBLE REVELATION AS REALIZED IN THE BRAHMINICAL PERIOD

CHAPTER VI.

THE TWO REVELATIONS AS IN THE *SRIMAT BHAGAVAT GEETA*.

CHAPTER VII.

THE *DARSHANAS*, AS THEY BEAR UPON THE TWO REVELATIONS.

CHAPTER VIII.

CHAPTER IX.

MISCELLANEOUS

CHAPTER I

Section 1:—Science and Art in Religion.

Science and Art as explained in the Introduction are twin sisters in every department of mental culture. In fact the whole of modern civilization consists of the two. In cultivating knowledge of the material world, one portion of the study is distinctly *scientific*, and another portion a matter of *art*. Take for instance the study of Chemistry; what is studied in the class-room in the shape of learning principles, laws and formulæ is Science. What is done in the laboratory is Art. As regards the cultivation of the knowledge of the mental and moral sphere of life, it may not be usual to carry on studies separately on the two lines, but it may be so carried on and aught to be. There are men however who would grudge to give religion a *locus standi* of its own in the sphere of *science* and *art*. They, however, are ready to test it by the data and facts of physical science, with a view to dismiss it as something baseless: But many would willingly admit the claim of religion to be the subject of science on its on *data* and facts. But a mere science of religion is a thing too lame to represent the whole truth of what is called religion. To represent the whole truth of it, the experience of those who practise religion should be put side by side with the science of religion. In other words religious Science and religions Art should go together in order to substantiate the truth of religion. In fact, it is the *art* of religion which is *religion proper*. For, the word religion without any qualification means the experiences of a man of religion. If one wants to test the truths of religion, he must honestly and earnestly ascertain not only the soundness of certain propositions and postulates affecting religion, but the force and result of what one experiences in practising religion. In medicine the clinical experience is often more useful than theoritical descriptions, in determining the properties of a drug. If one knows the science regarding an object, he only *knows* the qualities and character of that object. But one who has reduced the qualities of the object to some practical purpose in the shape of an Art, has *appreciated* and *felt* it. For instance, if one knows the science of heat, he is no doubt able to discuss about heat. But it is quite a different thing to be able to produce heat and fire. This requires some sort of tactics and experience which may be called the art of producing heat. Such tactics and experience may be various, but it is either by actually producing fire or by feeling it by touch that a man gets actual experience of what fire is. The scientist knows that every substance contains heat in it. But the practical man who requires fire, actually gets it produced by some shift or other, say, by rubbing two pieces of wood. This is *art* causing an effect which cannot but be home-felt and real. Similarly one may have knowledge of the science of chemistry without ever having been in the laboratory. Such a person can have no experience of chemical action, though he may have a knowledge of some of its laws. Take again the case of electricity. A scientific knowledge of electricity no doubt widens the range of human knowledge regarding nature. But it is the various electric arts to which mankind owes the manifold blessings of modern civilization.

Thus a complete treatment of a particular religious system must involve a consideration of the *science* portion and the *art* portion of that religious system. In many systems the two factors are not distinctly recognized. But the Hindu System distinctly recognises the dual phase and this recognition is the distinguishing feature of it.

Section 2.—Science and Art in Religion correspond to Rationalism and Emotionalism.

Roughly speaking, Rationalism is the developing of knowledge, and Emotionalism is the moving of the heart. And what are Science and Art as explained before? Science is clear knowledge, and Art is a practical appreciative movement. Thus generally speaking, Science corresponds to Rationalism and Art to Emotionalism. It is specially so in the case of religion, and as regards the Hindu religion, the distinction between Rationalism and Emotionalism as corresponding to *science* of religion and *art* of religion is brought out in relief at every step.

Rationalism and Emotionalism in ordinary parlour may simply mean reasoning and feeling processes as found in the lives of men in general. They may be simply matters of *loukika* (wordly) experience as the Hindus would say. But in the Hindu mind, the terms *Jnana* and *Bhakti* meaning Rationalism and Emotionalism convey a much higher import.*

Jnana is not common knowledge, but it is the illumination of the soul by which the *Para Brahma* is realized as the great Soul of the Universe. And *Bhakti* is similarly not an ordinary feeling of love and attachment, but that self-less devotion which the touch of the All-Beautiful and All-Loving Supreme

---

* संज्ञायते येन तदस्तदोषं
शुद्धं परं निर्म्मलमेकरूपम् ।
Vishnu Puran (6-5-60).

तत्प्राप्तिहेतुर्ज्ञानञ्च कर्म्म प्रोक्तं महामुने ।
Vishnu Puran (6-5-87).

Spirit draws-forth from the hearts of men.

Such is the Rationalism and Emotionalism of Hinduism so called. The process which leads to the above *Jnana* and *Bhakti* are respectively the process of purified Rationalism and Emotionalism.

Rationalism is sometimes associated with what is called *Nibritti* (renunciation) and Emotionalism with what is called *Prabritti* (activity).*

This association is not improper considering the concomitants of the two processes as shown below.

As stated above, Rationalism as inculcated by the Hindus, is knowledge purified. But how is it to be purified? It is purified by self-abnegation and abstraction. For, if self-seeking pre-dominates in any degree, it vitiates thought with prejudice. Thought is also subject to vitiation when one is in a whirlpool of excitement. Therefore self-abnegation and abstraction which are all

---

* द्वाविमावथ पन्थानौ यत्र वेदाः प्रतिष्ठिताः ।
प्रवृत्ति-लक्षणे धर्म्मौ निवृत्तिौ च विभाषितः ॥

Sankara-bhasya Bajeseneva Sanhita.

that is meant by the word renunciation, are associated with *Jnanakanda*. In other words, it is for this reason that *Jnanakanda* is said to be the *Nibritti Dharma*. Again, Emotionalism as approved by the Hindus, is similarly desire and action purified. But how are they to be purified? Desire and action cannot be purified by rest and inactivity. They cannot be altogether suppressed successfully or with any beneficial result. They are purified only by indulging in activity, in a self-sacrificing spirit. Thus, a self-sacrificing spirit of activity being the only means of purifying them, Emotionalism is very properly associated with what is called *Prabritti-Dharma* or proper indulgence in action.

In reality, there is no conflict between what is called *Nibritti Dharma* and what is called *Prabritti Dharma*. For *Nibritti* is the elimination of self-fulness and not the elimination of action.

Rationalism and Emotionalism may be compared and contrasted as follows :—The one is based upon *Viveka* or dispassionate analysis, the other upon *Sadhana* or earnest devotion.

The *quantum* of the one is measured by the extent, the *quantum* of the other is measured by the depth ; and thus the one tends to a conciousness of an all pervading expan sion, and the other tends to that of concentration to a point or to a focus.

The one widens the range of the view of the Divinity ; the other intensifies the touch of the Divinity.

The one imparts religious thoughts ; the other substantiates religious facts. In short, the great difference between Rationalism and Emotionalism is that, the one is of the theoretical character and the other of a practical character.

Rationalism or *science* supplies bare knowledge, but Emotionalism or *art* fulfils some want of the heart. Thus the truth of Rationalism is abstract, while the truth of Emotionalism is homefelt.

Although *science* and *art* are allied together, the function of each is separable. Similarly, the functions of Rationalism and Emotionalism are seperable ; the one gives an abstract knowledge of the Diety, and the other makes Him touched and felt in His protection and love.

Section 3 :—Rationalism and Emotionalism as Natural and Scriptural Revelations

Rationalism and Emotionalism are the means of revealing many spiritual truths and spiritual facts. So they may be called Natural Revelations. Again Rationalism and Emotionalism are distinctively taught in the Vedas. Therefore, as so taught they are scriptural Revelations. As Natural Revelations they are respectively called *Paramartha Tattwa* or *Tattwa Jnana* and *Paramartha Sadhan* or *Bhaktimarga.* As Scriptural Revelations they are respectively called *Jnana Kanda* and *Karma Kanda.* *

The expression *Karma Kanda* used with reference to the Vedas is synonymous with the expression *Bhakti Kanda* as used in other sacred books.

The *Jnanakanda* chiefly consists of the

---

* वेदस्तावत् काण्डद्वयात्मकः। तत्रपूर्व्वस्मिन् काण्डे नित्यनैमित्तिककाम्यनिषिद्धरूपं चैतुर्व्विधं कर्म्म

Upanishadas, which form the basis of the Religious philosophy or the Divine Science of the Hindus. The *Karmakanda* consists of the hymns and the *Mantras* which coupled with the prescribed forms of the *Jnanas* make what may be called the scriptural Art or the practical religion of the ancient Hindus. *

In the period called the Brahmanical period in which the *Smritis* came to be the guide of the practical life of the community, Hinduism presented the same dual aspect. Since the begining of this period the result of the *Jnanakanda* has been, to a great extent, reduced to forms and formulae such as the *Pranava* or the *Onkar* and the Gayatri. But side by side with this element of the

---

प्रतिपाद्यं ॥

*　　*　　*　　*　　*　　*　　*

तस्मादुत्तरकाण्डे ब्रह्मोपदेश-ब्रह्मोपास्तिश्चेतुत्रभयं प्रतिपाद्यते ॥

Taittriya Upanishata (1-1-1).

* कर्म्मकाण्डो ज्ञानकाण्ड इति भेदो द्विधा मतः ।

Siva Sanhita (1-20).

Jnanakanda (or Rationalism) the stream of *Karmakanda* (or Emotionalism) has been steadily flowing and expanding in the shape of that earnest and soul-stirring religion which consists in reverence and worship of the Supreme Being as Narayana or Vishnu.

The Bhagabat Geeta treats of the two sections of Hinduism presenting them in a philosophical as well as in a practical light. It shows the relative position of the two as *Jnana Yoga* and *Bhakti Yoga* broadly corresponding respectively to *Sankhya Yoga* and *Karma Yoga*. Then again, that fast and sharp line of demarcation which exists between the Darshanik Works and the Pauranic Works, both of comparatively later date, is the self-same demarcation between the *Jnanakanda* and the *Kamakanda*. The Darshanas (systems of philosophy) headed by the Vedanta give a strict scientific shape to the *Jnana*. The Puranas, on the other hand, illustrate the *Bhaktikanda* and *Karmakanda* in glowing poetical colours.

Thus Hinduism has always presented itself in a double aspect, the aspect of *Jnana*, and the aspect of *Bhakti* and *Karma*.

Section 4 :—What does Rationalism and Emotionalism severally reveal.

Says Sankhya, * " Nature is to make free the ever-free man. " Similarly one may say Rationalism and Emotionalism make evident —the self-evident Supreme Being. They reveal the Self-reavealed one. Take first Rationalism. How does it reveal the Supreme Being ? It does this step by step as follows according to the Hindu Shastras :—

First by the well-known *neti neti* (not this, not this) eliminating process, the reasoning facutly of man arrives at the conception of two ultimate entities—the conception of an All-knowing and All-witnessing Universal Soul pervading the Universe, and the conception, taking the Sankhya view of the matter, of an All-active physical Energy side by side with the same.

---

* विमुक्तमोचार्थं स्वार्थं वा प्राधानस्य ॥

(Sankhya Sutra-I-Bk II).

Then it becomes obvious to reason that the All-active dead physical energy is subservient to the All-knowing Universal Soul and is merely an environment to the latter. * So says the Sankhya who assumes a hostile attitude towards religion.

The physical energy however practically merges in the conscious Supreme Being, as Sankhya † itself admits, and Vedantists regard it as mere shadow—*mâyâ*—of the latter.

Thus reason arrives at the conception of one Supreme Being—*Para Brahma*—without a second—*Ekamevadwitiyam*.

Here reason halts for a moment. (See the Sankhya Philosophy). It puts the question: The *Para Brahma* may be All-knowing and All-witnessing, but is it the Supreme-Will Power—the *Ishwara*? But reason itself answers the question in a moment. Para Brahma having been proved to be all in all,

---

* संहतपरार्थत्वात् ॥

Sankhya Sutra—138-Bk. I.

† नोभयञ्च तत्त्वाख्याने ।

Sankhya Sutra—105. Bk. I.

to whom physical energy is but a shadow, it is necessarily the Supreme Will Power—the Ishwara.

Thus Rationalism reveals the Supreme Being not only as the All-knowing and All-witnessing but also as the All-powerful Supreme Will.

Next, what about his All pervading Love and Goodness? Reason is not forward to answer the question. But following once more the same eliminating process *neti* and *neti*, reason is forced to admit that in the vast load of pleasure and pain pressing upon the animal kingdom and the human race, pain has a vanishing tendency, for it is remedial. Thus pure bliss looms in the view of reason as the ultimate residuam of all pain and pleasure.

Thus Ratioinalism reveals the All-knowing, All-powerful, and All-loving Supreme Being— *Satchidānanda—Satyam-Jnanam-Anandam.*

But yet the whole as presented above is more or less skeleton like. How is the Supreme Being—the *Ishwarā*—the all in all of a man? How is God the resort of man's consolation, the great bank from which he can draw strength beyond measure? To answer all these questions—the Revelation of Emotionalism comes in. Says Emotionalism: we men are now so many scattered individuals—each individualized by the cover of a gross body. Take off these bodily covers which are transient, and we all merge into the All-knowing, All-powerful, All-loving Supreme Soul. Nay I become Himself—*Soham*. This is experimentally proved by Yoga or *Samâdhi*. Why then should I suffer and fear?

But even if a man cannot go up so high, let him try what is known as *Pratika Upâsanâ*—worshipping and praying to the Infinite One, by identifying Him with some Finite Work, or finite portion of His Universe, as when one worships Fire, or the overshadowing atmosphere (Varuna), as the Supreme God, or when he worships the personality of a man or the picture of the motherland as *Avatâr*. That the Supreme Being responds even to such worship and prayer is evident by the actual experience of those who make such worship and offer such prayer. For he gets strength and comfort—things substantial,—and can what is substantial proceed from what is unsubstantial? What is real cannot come from unreal. * This is the revelation of Emotionalism.

If you say that one does not see God personally : why not? He is seen in our heart of hearts though not with our physical eyes.

We believe that the Earth moves round the sun. Do we see it? No. On the other hand we see the contrary. Yet we believe it as firmly as if we actually saw it.

The above I have put as the *natural* revelation of *Jnan* and *Bhakti*. But in reality, they are as well the truths of *Scriptural* Revelation the *Jnan kânda* and *Karma Kanda* of the *Sruti*, and *Jnan Yoga* and *Bhakti Yoga* of the Geeta. No man need go beyond these Scriptural Revelations for any of his spiritual wants.

Section 5.—The Revelation of "Jnana" and "Bhakti" in its simple state—in relation to Universal religion.

There is a secular religion of the whole world—if that expression is allowable—as

---

* नासतो विद्यते भावः ।

Bhagabat Geeta.

contradistinguished from ecclesiastical religions of various countries.

The secular religion of all countries and of all nations is one and the same, embodying the first truths of the Vedanta in a simple form.

The ecclesiastical religion of every country and of every nation is different from each other—each containing peculiar colours and peculiar associations of its own in addition to the simple truths of *Jnan* and *Bhakti*. For instance in Christian countries there is the commonsense religious creed and sentiment of an Omnipotent, Omniscent and All-loving God, in whom men look for, and find consolation and help, apart from the peculiar doctrines and peculiar associations of Christianity. These peculiar doctrines and peculiar associations forms the ecclesiastical religion of the Christian nations, enforced more or less by the clergy, and in some places by the State. But the simple commonsense faith, which I have called the seculiar religion, is in the mouth and heart of the people at large, high and low, and find expressions in exclamations, literary writings, and in connection with the worldly business of the people. It is the same with the Mahammadans also. In appeals which a Mahammadan would make to Khoda or Allah, at times of sorrow and joy, in streets and bazars and in places of business, in fact on all occasions, other than those appointed and prescribed for prayer and sacrifice, they little think of any peculiar doctrine of the Koran. Similar is the case with the Hindus. When a Hindu in common matters of life, expresses his thanks to the Almighty, or expostulates with him for any seeming injustice, his mind is a clean sheet as regards the peculiar philosophical doctrines and prescribed forms of worship and prayer of his *Shastras*. Even as regards nations and countries, thought to be backward, and in a primitive state of society, such as Sonthals, Ourans, and the like, the same is the case. Their worship and prayer are peculiar to a degree of eccentricity. But when in fear they invoke Divine help, or in joy express gratitude to the Heaven, their utterances clearly indicate that they are thinking of the All-powerful and All-knowing God of the Universe. Thus, this floating religion of the world, which I have called the secular religion, is Hindu Vedantism in its pure and simple shape. But the ecclesiastical religion of every country has many differentiating features of its own, and these consists of colourings and associations, which make such religions not only different from each other, but sometimes arrayed in hostile attitude towards each other.

Though the ecclesiastical religion of any community should not be disregarded by the members of that community, yet it is proper to point out the comparative advantages and disadvantages of such religion, compared with the common-sense universal religion.

The ecclesiastical religion ensures a greater depth of devotional feeling ; but it is apt to lead to narrow sectarianism and bigotry. Again the rational features of religion are reduced to practical formulæ in ecclesiastical religion so as to ensure regularity and uniformity. But those formulæ run the risk of being reduced to dead ceremonials. Such are the advantages and disadvantages of the ecclesiastical religion as compared with the common-sense universal religion.

CHAPTER II.

Particular Features of Hinduism.

Section I:—The Scientific Study of the Hindu Religion.

The scientific study of the Hindu religion embraces the study of the Vedanta and the Sankhya. No doubt, the Vedanta purports to be only the interpretation of the *Sruti*, but by the very definition of Sruti, as distinguished from *Linga* and *Vakya*, it consists of such texts of the Vedas, as carry conviction of their truth, as soon as they are heard or pronounced. Therefore the question of conviction comes in, even in interpreting the Vedas and it becomes necessary to present them in such a light as to make the truths contained therein self-evident. In other words it is necessary to present them in the light of the highest reason in man and that is what Badarayan has done in the Vedanta *Sutras*. This makes the Vedanta Darshana a Science —though it is a science of the revealed truths.

—whether read in the light of the commentaries of Sankaracharya or of Ramanuja.

The Sankhya on the other hand takes up a position, which in these days would be called the position of a positivist. His discussions and arguments are all of a purely scientific character. But they end in a way which far from dissatisfying the prophets of religion, has been earnestly welcomed by them. In fact the Sankhya Philosophy imparts a strictly scientific character to the Hindu religion.

Both the Vedanta and the Sankhya are at one that by the process of eliminiting the accidental from the essential,—the *neti-neti* process—one arrives at the conception of the All-knowing and All-witnessing Universal Soul. The Sankhya recognises the fact that the soul as individualized by means of bodies is multitudinous. * But this makes no cardinal difference from the Vedanta according to which *Upâdhi* (environment) makes a variety of existence as regards the *Atman*. But the

---

* जन्मादिव्यवस्थातः पुरुषवहुत्वम् ॥

Sankhya—Sutra—147. Bk- I.

Sankhya conception of the Universal Soul (not individualized) is as distinct from the conception of the *individualized Purusa*, as that of the Universal Soul of the Vedanta is from the conception of the soul as variagated by *Upâdhi* (environment). In dealing with the question of proof, the Sankhya makes a distinction between what is proof of the *Purusha* (individualized soul) and what of the *Atman* (universal soul). He says :—"The *Atman*—Universal Soul—exists because there is no proof to the contrary." * But of the *Purusha* (individualized soul) he says :—"That and Prakriti are both proved by the common proofs dealt with by him." †

"Again in *Sutra* (116-Bk. V) he says :—the Purusha realizes the conception of *Brahma* in a state of *Samâdhi* etc."‡ This is

---

* अस्त्यात्मा नास्तित्वसाधनाभावात् ॥

Sankhya—Sutra 1. Bk. VI.

† उभयसिद्धिः प्रमाणात्तदुपदेशः ।
सामान्यतोदृष्टादुभयसिद्धिः ॥

Sankhya—Sutra, 100 & 101, Bk. I.

‡ समाधिसुषुप्तिमोक्षेषु ब्रह्मरूपता ॥

Sankhya—Sutra 116—Bk. V.

a distinct recognition of the conception of the *Brahma*—the Universal Soul—as a separate conception from that of the Purusha (the individualized soul).

Really when one remembers, how on the subject of the cosmic evolution Kapila Deva speaks of the Purusha on the one hand, and of the Prakriti on the other ; it becomes clear that in this connection, he is not speaking of the many individualized purushas, but of the Universal Soul.

Thus there is no difference between the Vedanta and the Sankhya, so far as the conception of the All-knowing and All-witnessing Universal Soul is concerned. The seeming difference begins with the question—Is the All-knowing and All-witnessing Universal Soul, merely All-knowing and All-witnessing, or, is it also the All-will and All-powerful *Ishwara* ?

The question having arisen at first in connection with the correctness of the Sankhya definition of direct perception, Kapila Dev says :—'If you mean by *Ishwara* a localised existence ; I say that there is no such existence fit to be called *Ishwara*, as in addition to the bound man, and to the liberated man, there is no third existence of the kind." * But the author says nothing here with reference to the conception of the All-knowing and All-witnessing Universal Soul being the All-will and All-powerful Supreme One. The subject of this conception, the Sankhya takes up latter on. Having shewn that even the individualized soul when merged in the First Cause, comes out as the Active † he says that He—the *Para-atmá*—‡ is All-knowing and All-will. And then—apprently remembering that on a former occasion he said

---

* ईश्वरासिद्धे : (न दोष) ; (See Sutra 89)

Sankhya-Sutra 92—Bk. I.

मुक्तबद्धयोरन्यतराभावान्न तत्सिद्धिः ॥

उभयथाप्यसत्करत्वम् ॥

Sankhya-Sutra 93 & 94—Bk. I.

† न कारणलयात् कृतकृत्यता मग्नवदुत्थानात् ।

अकार्य्यत्वेऽपि तद् योगः पारवश्यात् ॥

Sankhya-Sutra 52, 53—Bk. III.

‡ पर आत्मा किंरूप इत्यत्राह ।

Anirudha Bhatta.

सहि सर्ब्बवित् सर्ब्बकर्त्ता ॥

Sankhya-Sutra 54—Bk. III.

that the *Ishwara* was not proved in a certain way he adds—"such proof of *Ishwara* is verily the sound proof."* The word ईदृश (such) evidently refers to सिद्धि (proof) and not to *Ishwara*. For the transcedental character of the Sankhya conception of *Ishwara* is clearly indicated by the Sutras 93 and 94, Bk. I. in which he demurs to give the name of *Ishwara* to any limited existence. In fact Kapila Dev has never questioned that in the All-knowing and All-witnessing Universal Soul, lies the Supreme Will-power. In Sutra 99. Bk I. it is stated that the *Buddhi* gets its will-power, from the Atmâ, just as the iron gets heat from the fire. †

No doubt the Sankhya holds that in the case of man as he is, he is temporarily without any real will-power so long as he is engrossed with the sense of *egoism* (selffulness). ‡ While he is so engrossed, he is a slave to

---

* ईदृशेश्वरसिद्धिः सिद्धा ।
Sankhya.Sutra—57. Bk. III.

† अन्तःकरणस्य तदुज्ज्वलितत्वाल्लोहवदधिष्ठातृत्वम् ।
Sankhya-Sutra—99. Bk. I.

‡ अहङ्कारः कर्त्ता न पुरुषः ।
Sankhya—Sutra—54—Bk. VI.

forces extraneous to him by way of *Karma*, which fosters this sense of egoism (self fulness). However he shows that man regains his lost will-power as soon as he is freed from this egoism (self fulness) by being merged in the First Cause (See Sutra 52, 53. Bk. III quoted before).

Thus all that the Sankhya says regarding the paramount activity of Prakriti, has reference to the conditon of man in the state of *karmabandha* ; in other words it has reference to that condition of man, in which he surrenders his will-power to Prakriti by *aviveka*—ignorance and confusion. But by *Viveka*, namely, conciousness that man is inseparable from the All-knowing, All-witnessing, All-will and All-powerful *Atmâ*, he regains his full will-power and full knowledge, and is thus saved from the shackles of *karma*, which makes him a mere creature of circumstances. The moral of the law of *karma* is beautifully explained by Sankhya in Sutra 7—Bk. II which says :—"As one puts thorns in the way of a man, to make him weary, so is this working of *karma*."* The Vedanta

---

* "चेतनोद्देशान्नियमः कण्टकमोक्षवत्" ॥
Sankhya—Sutra—7—Bk. II.

would call the law of *karma* as *Mâyâ*—something nothing. It is something when man is engrossed by *avidya*. It is nothing when *Jnan* is obtained. The conclusion arrived at by the Yoga Shastra, the Naya and the Vaisheshika are practically the same. The Bhagabat Geeta and the Mahabharata take Sankhya Phillosophy to be as represented above. The views of commentators to the contrary cannot outweigh the view taken in these sacred books.

Section 2 :—How practically the truths of the Hindu religion are experienced.

To experience the truths of religion by practice, is the highest art of human life. The practice of *Yoga* and the worship by *mantra*, as followed by the Hindus are the best illustrations of it.

Yoga and the principle of worship by *mantra* both have an introduction in the Vedanta. *Sravana*, *manana*, and *nididhyasana* of the Vedanta Darshana are nothing but *Yoga* in a general form ; while the teachings of *Pratika-Upâsanâ* in it inculcates the great principle of worship by *mantra*. The Patanjal Darshana elaborates the principle of *Yoga*. The Mimansa Darshana brings out in detail the great principle of worship by *mantra*. In both of these the basical element is devotion — *Pranidhâna* — to *Ishwara*. Both of these are means of obtaining the higher will-power man is capable of.

The *Yoga* practically illustrates that great truth, faintly indicated by the expression—*Nature abhors vacuum*. The proper expression is,—Take away the gross and the fine comes in, to occupy its place. Remove the dross of the world and the divine light of the highest religious truths fills up the gap. So what is called *Yoga*—union—begins with *Biyoga*—disunion. But the law by which the dispersion of the dross is followed by the presence of the fine, abstractly is a law of force. Burn the wood and you get the force of heat. So abstractly *Yoga* is the law for generating force. The direction of the force may vary. The force engendered may temporarily be used for undesirable purposes. Therefore it is necessary that precaution should be taken to secure a proper direction of the force. And this precaution is made imparative by Patanjala by laying down *Yama*—moral control, *Niyama*—moral practices—as the first steps of *Yoga* ; and also by requiring that *Yoga* should begun by act of devotion and self denial, *Ishwara Pranidhâna* and *Tapas*.* The wonderful effects of *Yoga*, —the grand experience it brings, can be realized by practice and practice alone. In short as Patanjala shows that not only the channel of inspiration—*Pratibhâ*—is perenially opened by *Yoga*, but that in the end one finds himself posted in the fort of will-power —*Chiti-Sakti*—when the *guuas* of *Prakriti* being disarmed of all noxious tendency cannot in the least heart him.†

The great principle of *mantra* is brought out by the Mimansa Darshana as an upshot of *Pratika Upâsanâ*. It solves the difficulty

* तपःस्वाध्यायेश्वरप्रणिधानानि क्रियायोगः ।

Patanjala—Sutra 1—Bk. II.

† पुरुषार्थशून्यानां गुणानां प्रतिप्रसवः। कैवल्यं स्वरूपप्रतिष्ठा वा चितिशक्तिरिति ॥

Patanjala—Sutra 34—Bk. IV.

of realizing the *Infinite*, by means of the *finite*. The word *mantra* means that by which the mind is saved, *i. e.* taken out of its own narrow grooves.

There is *something* in the mind of man by which it can transcend itself, by which the *finite* as itself it is, is put in the way of the Infinite. Realization of that *something* is *mantra*. The medium or body of a *mantra* consists of words or sounds. An earnest will impressed upon words makes those words as powerful as the earnest will itself. The hymns of the Rigveda and the songs of the Shyamveda and the formulæ of the Yoyurveda are *mantras*. The hymns and songs addressed initially to the finite powers of Nature—the Agni, Baruna, Mitra and the like called *devatâs*, are all but earnest expressions of the heart and mind of man, directed to the Infinite One, and they do go up to the Infinite One. The language of the hymns and songs show this on the face of them. Says the Mimansha—the *devatâs* are *Mantravarnika* (colouring by *mantras*.) .This practically means that they are mere pegs on which *matras* hang. The *mantras*—the upheaval of man's mind and heart to the most High—forms the essence of the whole thing, and as such, in them lies the power of salvation. In fact generally speaking *mantras* work wonders and miracles provided they are directed to some noble object, and with devotion—*Pranidhâna*—to *Ishwara*. So noble objects are fulfilled by *mantras*, when with *Ishwara* as the goal, it embodies a resolution such as "Fulfilment of the object or let life go."

Thus the two salient features of Hinduism are the *Yoga Vidya* and the *Mantra Vidya*—the two blessed arts for stirring and elevating the human soul and identifying it with the Supreme Soul. The word *Vidya* as in *Yoga Vidya*, requires a word of explanation. In the ancient works the words *Vidya* and *Jnana* are used not in an identical sense. In Vedanta Darshana, *Vidya* is used in the sense of the highest art, while *Jnana* in the sense of the highest knowledge. That differentiation of meaning is illustrated by the fact that Ganesh is known as the God of knowledge, *(Jnana)*; while Saraswati as the Goddess of Fine-arts *(Vidya)*. However that may be, the *Yoga Vidya* and the *Mantra Vidya* do not form the highest phase of Emotionalism, which is the *Bhakti Yoga.* By *Yoga* and *Mantra* the Divine powers in man are cultivated. But by *Bhakti Yoga* in the shape of the *Srikrishna Lilâ* or of *Devi Lilâ*, Divine love in man is cultivated. The songs and hymns of the Vaishnavas—the *Mahâjan Padas*—and those of Devi-worshippers, such as composed by Ram Prasad of Bengal, need not be compared with the *Mantras* of the Vedas, for such comparison is not proper.

Now a word about the old habit of polemical discussions over such words as *Sâkâra, Nirâkâra* and *Saguna* and *Nirguna*. These discussions and controversies are the relics of the old scholastic age. It is high time now, that no energy should should be lost over these discussions. Suffice it to say as regards the question of *Sâkâr* and *Nirâkâr*, that religious consciousness is the consciousnes of the Finite, opening into the Infinite and of the Infinite narrowing into the Finite. There is no consciousness of the Infinite without reference to the Finite, and there is no consciousness possible of finding the last limit of the Finite. Thus the Supreme Being is the Infinite, narrowing into the Finite, and the Finite opening into the Infinite. When the devotee refering to a particular form *(akâr)*, says,—'this is my God' he is bound to add,—'it is the focus of the Infinite.'

Similarly when one referring to an abstract eliminating conception says,—'my God is without form' he is bound to add,—'these are His limited manifestations.' Thus from the nature of things, the Supreme Being is both *Nirâkarâ* and *Sâkâra*.

Again as regards the question of *Saguna* and *Niguna*, it has been seen before, that both the *science* side and the *art* side of the Hindu religion establish that God is '*Satchidânand*' *(Satyam, Jnanam, Anandam)*—the Absolute Truth, the Absolute Intelligence, and the Absolute Bliss. Thus *guna* being relative, God is *Nirguna*. But He is not untruth, unintelligent, unblessed. This at least makes him *Saguna*—not to speak of the necessity of the *Gunas* in *Dhyana*, *Dhâranâ* and in *Pratika Upâsanâ*.

Now one sees what Hinduism is. Taking

the two sides—the rational or the *science* side and the emotional or the *art* side—together, Hinduism is in one view a complex system, but in another view, it is the simplest of all systems. Of other nations religion is a thing—a part. But of the Hindu nation it is its whole existence

Sree Bhagvata Geeta puts all the truths, tenets, and precepts of Hinduism, in the clearest and the most telling light. That Scripture is enough for the people to follow. The Dharmashâstras constitute the social code of the nation, embodying the results of the Hindu system of socialism. These Shâstras should not be confounded with the Hindu system of Religious science and art. The Hindu Ethical system, consisting of the principles of the *Pravritti* and *Nibritti* Dharma, in the light of the *gunas*—*Sattwa*, *Rajas* and *Tamas*—should not also be mixed with the subject of Hindu religion proper.

Section 3 :—Hinduism teaching how the dry light of Science is the healing balm of Salvation.

Two of the great exponents of Hinduism, Gautama and Kanâda, demonstrate how the ordinary methods of logic and physical science end in revealing the great truths of religion. Rishi Gautama shows that the logic of thought is the logic of ethics and religion. Rishi Kanâda shows that the ways of physics is the way of metaphysics and faith. At first sight these may appear paradoxical. But a proper study of the works of these two great authors leaves no doubt that what they say is true.

First the *Naya Darshana*. To take the word *naya* of the Hindus, as meaning merely formal logic is an eggregious mistake. The word *naya* means the way in which one concrete truth leads to another truth. It is not confined to explaining a law of thought. It does that and goes far beyond it. It shows how the truth of a general proposition*—such

* यत्सिद्धावन्यप्रकरणसिद्धिः सोऽधिकरणसिद्धान्तः ।

Sutra—30. Sec 1—Chap. I.
Naya Darshana.

as 'where there is smoke, there is fire' is to be established, from which minor propositions may be derived as corrolaries from it,—such as 'the mountain is in fire because there is smoke.'

But the modern system of logic assumes the existence of the truth of the general proposition—the major premise—and shows how after that assumption, the course of reasoning should proceed.

But according to Gautama the more important question is, how the truth, of the major premise can be determind, than the question how assuming its truth, further reasoning is to proceed. The former question is the question of the *Vyapti (Sarvatantra.)** In the case of the illustration referred to, the question of *Vyapti (Sarvatantra)* is whether it is true that wherever there is smoke there is fire. In other words is fire the *Vyapaka*, and smoke the *Vyapta* ?

The means of determining the *Vyapti* constitute the more essential part of Hindu

* सर्वतन्त्राविरुद्धस्तन्त्रेऽधिकृत्तोर्थः सर्वतन्त्रसिद्धान्तः

Sutra—28 Sec 1—Chap. I.
Naya Darshana.

naya than the course of reasoning to be adopted assuming the *Vyapti.*

According to Europeans, the truth of the general proposition—the major premise—is left to be established by an extentensive observation and induction.

But says the Hindu *Naiyaik*—'the collection of a vast number of instances is often impracticable. Besides where there is such a collection even then it is not conclusive.'

So Gautama would in addition to observation and induction *(Prattakshya and Anumâna)* suggest analogy *(Upamâna)* and testimony *(Sabda)*,—such testimony as commands reverence and faith—as the proper means of testing the truth of a *Vyapti* proposition.

But further Gautama, while admitting the utility of argument and discussions between persons taking up opposite sides of a question, insists that there should be a fair and bonâfide spirit of enquiry and no *Jalpa*, *Chala* and *Jati.* Such a spirit of enquiry does often half the work of *pramâna* (proof). This is the *naya* (logic) of *Gautama*, as regards the investigation of physical truths. His *naya* extends also to the investigation of moral truths

Now what is his *naya* (logic) of Ethics? His *naya* of Ethics, equally with his *naya* of thought requires the establishment of the *Vyapti* or the major premise. No one denies that the human mind is bound to make a distinction as that between right and wrong—*Sreya* and *Heya*. But inorder to determine whether a particular act is right or wrong, the process adopted is similar to that required in determining whether the mountain is with fire, because of the smoke. As in determining this latter question it is necessary to establish the *Vyapti*—'wherever there is smoke, there is fire', so inorder to determine whether an act is right, it is necessary to establish some general proposition of right and wrong to serve as a major premise. And such a major premise must be established almost in the same way as a major premise in the sphere of physical truth. The only difference being that while in the case of the formar there is more of observation and induction, in the case of the latter there is more of *Sraddhâ*, —spontaneous regard—which is involved in the means of proof called *Sabda*—unimpeachable precepts. When a general moral proposition is established in the shape of an ethical *Vyapti*, whether a particular act is covered by it or not is easily determined. For instance there is the *Vyapti* or major proposition "न हिंसयेत् ."—(*Na hinsayeta*) which is a precept of the Vedas. The question arises whether the sacrifice of an animal at *Yajna* is *hinsa*, within the meaning of the precept. If so it would be wrong to make the sacrifice. This is Gautama's *naya* —logic—of Ethics. It is thus, that the word *naya* is used in Sanskrit and in the vernaculars not simply as a means of determining the truth or otherwise of a physical proposition, but as the means of determining the righteousness or otherwise of an action.

Now as regards questions of the Godhead and the salvation, Gautama claims that these questions are intimately connected with the process of determining the truth of a proposition and the similar process of determining the righteousness of an action. The existence of the *Parama Atman* is self-evident. The *Srutis* declare it and no one disputes it. Even the Sankhya says—"the *Atman* exists because there is no proof to the contrary". But some people doubt whether the *Parama Atman* is *Ishwara i. e.* the Supreme Will by which the world has been created and which regulates it. To such men Gautama would indignantly say—'the mass of truth, physical and moral, established by the logic both of thought and ethics, establish the moral order of the Universe in which everything tends to show a Supreme Will.' In fact the whole Universe is what one may call the *Resgestæ* of a Supreme Will. Man requires consolation and peace. Without the Supreme will the want remains, and in fact becomes pressing at every step.

Therefore man feels that the Supreme Will—*Ishwara*,—is at the back of his limited will, and is comforted and consoled in respect of misfortunes to which he is subject.*

* ईश्वरः कारणं पुरुषकर्माफल्यदर्शनात्

Sutra—19 Sec 1—Chap. 4.

न पुरुष कर्माभावे फलानिष्पत्तेः

Sutra—20 Sec 1—Chap. 4.

तत्कारितत्वादहेतुः ।

Sutra—21 Sec 1—Chap. 4.

Naya Darshana.

Such comfort and consolation could not come from a hallucination. This is the *naya* philosophy. It will be seen that the *naya* argument is not open to the fault of what is known as the teleological argument. In short the whole programme of the *Naya Darshana* is to establish the Will Supreme or the Will of the *Ishwara* and to realize faith in the same.

Section 4 :—Hinduism teaching how the dry light of Science is the healing balm of Salvation. (Contd).

The Vaishesika Darshana similarly demonstrates that a proper analytical study of nature inevitably leads man to a peculiar faith, *(Dharma Vishesha)* which is the *sumum bonam* of his existence Rishi Kanâda maintains, that if one analytically studies the Universe, all that it contains would be found to consist of an infinite array of subtle atoms, the combinations of which would fall under six categories, viz.—things, qualities, actions, the general, the special and the concrete. Thus some atoms are the nucleus of substantiality, others of quality, and others of action. While some of these are more or less of a general character, others are of a special character ; and these combining form concrete objects.

The above analytical view of the study of Nature, presents a complete picture within a small compass of what are the essential elements of a scientific study. A study of the substances, qualities, and actions with reference to what is general and what is particular, show the necessary features of what is called by Europeans—physics and natural history, while a study of the details about the formation of concrete objects would cover the sphere of what is called Chemistry. The combination of the general and the the special in forming concrete things lead to normal and abnormal, (*Sadharma and Baidharma*) results as regards things, qualities and actions, *i. e.* Nature presents not only normal things, normal qualities and normal actions, but also abnormal. So the atoms let alone, would make the Universe a strange combination of the normal and abnormal. But the category of substances is headed by *manas* (mind) and Atman—the former having as its quality the human will-power (*Budhhi*) and the latter, *Atman*, the Will-power pervading everything.

To the human will-power, the conflict of the normal and the abnormal is oppressive. It must have a Supreme Will-power to appeal to for comfort and consolation, and it has this in the Paramatmana which is transcendental (unlike the human will-power).

Gautama shows that by the process of *Naya*, the mind in the first instance becomes well informed as regards physical truths; marking them from what is false; and then in the next place by a similar process it distinguishes between right and wrong, and eventually finds itself landed on a moral and spiritual order of Nature; face to face with the Supreme Will—*Ishwara*. Kanâda likewise shows that, at first the human mind becomes informed of physical substances, physical qualities and physical actions, and then perforce it is drawn to a higher plane of knowledge*,—knowledge of thought substances, thought qualities and mental actions—and further it cannot rest there, but is inevitably drawn to a plane of right and wrong action, in which plane the human mind comes in contact witha will, higher than ours†, and gets into absolute reliance on it‡, which proves itself the *summum bonum* of existence.

The impulse, which forces the mind from a lower plane to a higher, is called by Rishi Kanâda, '*Abhâva*' (want), *i, e.* a natural forcing up from a sense of urgent want. This *Abhâva-Pramana* is peculiar to the Vaishesika Darshana.

---

* इन्द्रियार्थप्रसिद्धिरिन्द्रियार्थेभ्योऽर्थान्तरस्य हेतुः ।

Sutra—2, Sec—1, Chap.—III
Vaishesika Darshana.

† संज्ञा कर्म्म त्वस्मद्विशिष्टानां लिङ्गम्
प्रत्यक्षप्रवृत्तत्वात् संज्ञाकर्म्मणः ।

Sutra—18 & 19, Sec—1, Chap.—II.
Vaishesika Darshana.

‡ विशिष्टे आत्मत्याग इति

Sutra—16, Sec—1, Chap.—VI.
Vaishesika Darshana.

Though credited with the doctrine of atoms this Darshana is called Vaisheshika, because the doctrine of the special as contrasted with the general, practically plays an important part in this philosophy, even more than the metaphysical doctrine of the atomic theory, as it is the special which leads to the abnormal, and as it is between the normal and the abnormal, that the human will-power (*Buddhi*) and the Supreme Will-power (*Ishwara*) are realized. The whole frame of the Vaisheshika Darshana is to establish the Supreme Will—*Ishwara*, an earnest and active faith in whom is salvation.

The great theological arguments of Rishis Kanâda and Gautama is founded upon the opposites—good and evil, which distract and worry man at every step of his existence. This conflict is in man's intellectual cognition, in his emotional experience and in his moral consciousness. The whole of nature presents to him this distracting and worrying conflict between good and evil. In man's intellectual cognition, it is in the shape of the truth and the false. In his emotional experience, it is in the shape of the pleasurable and painful. In his moral consciousness, it is in the shape of the right and the wrong. All this is visible nature. The whole effort of visible Nature is to rescue man from this sad dilemma. But nature goes only some way in this direction, and then abruptly falls short.* In fact its effort ends in merely indicating an urgent want. It leaves man tossed between the billows of good and evil, and merely prompts him towards a harbour which however is beyond its limits.

That harbour is the *Ishwara,* and when man reaches that harbour, he is at the end of his troubles and attains *Nissreyasa* (निः श्रेयसः) by the grace of *Ishwara.*†

---

* दृष्टानां दृष्टप्रयोजनानां दृष्टाभावे प्रयोगोऽभ्युदयाय

Sutra—8 Sec—2. Chap—X.

Vaisheshika Darshana.

† ईश्वरः कारणं पुरुषकर्माफल्यदर्शनात्

Sutra—19 Sec—1 Chap.—IV.

Naya Darshana.

CHAPTER III.

Detailed Observations as to how Rationalism and Emotionalism Reveal the Deity.

Section 1.—How Rationalism and Emotionalism Respectively bear on the subject of Personal God.

Emotionalism consists of personal affections. In its purified and exalted sphere, its very existence lies in the realization of the Supreme Personality, reigning in the Universe. Rationalism follows an impersonal eliminating process, in arriving at the existence of the Supreme Being. It eliminates the accidental, the changeable and the gross, until it gets at the permanent, the unchangeable and the spiritual Soul of all beings and things.* Thus it is apt to lose sight of the Supreme Personality reigning in the Universe. But this anti-

---

* अथात आदेशो नेति नेति नातः परमस्ति ।

Brihadaranyaka Upanishad.

thesis between the two cannot last. For, as the Universe teems with personal beings, pointing to a Central Personality as their origin, Rationalism too, is bound to admit the Supreme Being as the Central Personality of all personalities existing in the Universe.* Thus, even the Vedânta Darshana admits that creation implies intelligence and will, † and therefore a personal creator, just as Sreemat Bhagabat Geeta declares that above all other persons, is the Supreme person—the *Purushottama*—who is the Supreme Will and the Supreme Eternal Lord, entering all the *Lokas* and supporting them. ‡

---

* क्लेशकर्म्मविपाकाशयैरपरामृष्टः पुरुषविशेष ईश्वरः ।

Patanjala Sutra (1-24).

स पूर्वेषामपि गुरुः कालेनानवच्छेदात् ।

Ibid (1-26).

† ईक्षतेर्नाशब्दम् । *Vedanta Sutra (1-5).*

स ऐक्षत एकोऽहं बहु स्याम् प्रजायेय ।

Aitareya Upanishad.

‡ उत्तमः पुरुषस्त्वन्यः परमात्मेत्युदाहृतः ।

यो लोकत्रयमाविश्य बिभर्त्त्यव्यय ईश्वरः ॥

Geeta (15-17).

Thus Rationalism though starting with an impersonal eliminating process, reveals the Supreme Being both as personal and impersonal. * Even what is called the *Adwaitabâd* is not inconsistent with the idea that, all beings move and live in the Supreme Personality of the Universe just as the Bhagabat Geeta puts it, that the highest development of man appears then, when he sees the person of God in everything. † So far from the point of view of Rationalism.

Emotionalism, however, starts from the stand-point of person—the individual man. Man's personal wants and personal tendencies, all point to the Great Personality. His feelings become sickly, if not directed in the way of the Will of the Supreme Personality. They therefore seek to be consonant with the Supreme Will. That Will responds to

---

* द्वे ब्रह्मणी वेदितव्ये परञ्चापरञ्च ॥

Brihadarnyaka Upanishad.

† बहूनां जन्मनामन्ते ज्ञानवान् मां प्रपद्यते ।
वासुदेवः सर्वमिति स महात्मा सुदुर्लभः ॥

Geeta (7-19).

मयि सर्वमिदं प्रोतं सूत्रे मणिगणा इव ।

Geeta (7-7)-

man, and reciprocates love with love. Thus while the tendency of rationalism is, sometimes, to lose sight of the Supreme Personality, that of Emotionalism is to deepen and glorify the same. Of course, God is infinite and omnipotent to Emotionalism, as well as to Rationalism. Rationalism at the lowest does this service to religion: It shows that the world is not mere a collection of material forces, and that man is not mere a scum of earth.

Emotionalism, on the other hand, meets face to face the beautiful and loving God in the beauties and lovely works of Nature.

The revelation of Rationalism is the revelation of science and philosophy. That of Emotionalism is the revelation of history and poetry. Rationalism, through science, demonstrates God as the author of universal order and design. Through Philosophy, it shows that, He is the Supreme Soul and Supreme Essence.

Emotionalism, through History, realizes the bodily presence of God, in those sacred lives known as *Avatârs*; through poetry, it realizes His beauty and love in one or other prominently beautiful and lovely things of Nature. These associations of history and poetry, which gather round the presence of God in the mind of the Emotional worshipper, become inseparably associated with His presence, and are called His *leelas*.

But the field, where both Rationalism and Emotionalism directly display their revealing functions most prominently, is the mind and heart of each individual man. The individual, through *Jnana Yoga* (Rationalism), becomes conscious of the vast potentialities and latent powers of his soul, and thus comes to know the greatness of the Universal Soul.

Through *Bhakti Yoga* he realizes, how his own weak and tender self, is in need of the care and protection of One who is All-powerful and All-good, and how he actually finds such a One, by whom alone his littleness and ugliness can be consoled and cured. This All-powerful and All-good One—the personal God of Nature and the best relation of man is found in the vast expanse of impersonalities, by the art of *Sâdhanâ* and by the talisman of *Bhakti*.

These remove the cover of *Mâyâ* (the mystery of separation) which, according to rationalism, conceals God from the view of man.*

Bhakti knocks perseveringly and causes the cover of *Mâyâ* to remove itself from between the votary and his God. Thus the man of *Bhakti* finds the personal presence of his God at any spot, and in any form where and wherein he earnestly seeks Him.

Section 2—How Rationalism and Emotionalism bear on the subject of man's relations with the Deity.

The spiritual science of the Upanishads and the Vedanta discloses the moral and spititual order of the Universe, and the divine potentialities of man. The blessed art of *Sâdhanâ*, with *Bhakti*, discloses what the position of the individual

---

* पुरुषः स परः पार्थ भक्त्या लभ्यस्त्वनन्यया ।

Geeta (8-22).

नाहं प्रकाशः सर्वस्य योगमाया समावृतः ॥

Geeta (7-25).

man is, in that universal, moral and spiritual order, and how he can improve that position, by making closer the relation subsisting between him and the Lord of the Universe. Man, as a small moral machine in this world, is dependent upon many a moral relationship such as the parental, the filial, the conjugal and the like. But the father and the mother or the son or the husband or the like, are in existence to-day, to-morrow they are no more. Besides, they are all imperfect and full of failings. So, man, in order to be able to move on in the course of moral progress and of spititual development, stands in need of a perfect father or a perfect mother, ect., to help him on. By *Sâdhanâ* with *Bhakti* man gets such a father or mother in that Being by whose ordination he is made more or less to depend upon such relationships.* Thus while *Jnâna* reveals to man God, as the Supreme Spirit, the Supreme Being or the Supreme Soul, *Bhakti* reveals Him,

---

* आत्मानमेव प्रियमुपासीत। य आत्मानमेव प्रियमुपास्ते न हास्य प्रियं प्रमायुकं भवति ॥

Sutri.

as his Lord, Friend, Father, Mother and Lover.*

In the light of reason and abstract knowledge an individual man's relation with the rest of humanity, is that he is one of the same *genus*; that he and the rest of humanity have the same common physiology and the same common psychology. But in the light of emotion his relation with the rest of humanity is, that he is one of the same kith and kin; that he is one of an universal brotherhood. The common physiology and and psychology of the whole of humanity indicates a common Intelligential Power governing humanity. But the realization that, all men are of the same kith and kin, and that they form the same brotherhood, indicates a common Father, in whom the brotherly relation between man and man, has its basis and source.

Jnâna sees with a telescopic eye, *Bhakti* sees with a microscopic eye. *Jnâna* perceives the essence, *Bhakti* feels the sweetness.

---

* पिताहमस्य जगतो माता धाता पितामहः ।

Geeta (9-17).

Jnâna discovers the Supreme Intelligence, *Bhakti* reciprocates to the Supreme Loving Will.

Science, either spiritual or material, reveals power and force. But while the material sciences reveal some fine material force or power as pervading all matter, the spiritual science of the Hindus, the Upanishads, reveals the one Intelligential Force and the one All-powerful Will as pervading, ordering and controlling the whole Universe*—the *Para-Brahma* or the *Paramâtmâ*. But *Bhakti* (the spiritual art) which includes *Karma Yoga* as its issue, reveals the same *Para-Brahma* or *Paramâtmâ*, as centralized and personalised, in a sweet and approachable shape.

---

* एष सेतु र्विधरण एषां लोकानाम् असम्भेदाय ।

Brihadaranvaka Up.

भीषास्य पवनो वाति * * मृत्यु र्धावति पञ्चमः ।

Katha Upanishad.

मया ततमिदं सर्वं जगदव्यक्तमूर्त्तिना ।

Geeta (9-4).

स दाधार पृथिवीमुत द्याम् ।

Rigveda (10 Mandal).

The material arts lead to wonderful and happy results, arising from the combination of two or more material things with a set object and purpose. The spiritual art of *Karma Yoga* and *Bhakti* (purified action and feeling), lead to infinitely happier and infinitely more wonderful results, arising from setting your heart upon the Divine Grace. "Though Vishnu is present everywhere, no benefit is obtained from the Omnipresent Almighty God, unless one prays to Him."*

In fact, as already stated, the Revelation of *Jnâna* constitutes Religious Philosophy or Theosophy, while the Revelation of *Karma Yoga* and *Bhakti* constitutes Religion proper.

Section 3.—The Two Phases of Nature.

The Universe presents a double aspect It presents a rationalistic aspect and an artistic aspect. On the rational side of

---

* तथा विष्णुः शरीरस्थो न करोति हितं नृणाम् ।
विनाराधनया देवः सर्वगः परमेश्वरः ॥

Garura Purana (1-227-4).

Nature, man finds order, law, and intelligence; on the artistic side of it, he finds beauty and sublimeness, skill and love. Studying the rational side of Nature, one discovers a Supreme Intelligence pervading all things, and an universal spiritual essence underlying the whole world of accident or phenomena. This is Vedantism or the rational side of Hinduism. On the artistic side of Nature one meets with adaptation of means to particular ends, charming combinations, fine and nice displays of skill, all showing beauty, love and benevolence. When one is impressed with these, his heart swells with love and devotion, and is propelled to be a factor to swell the Universal current of love by his own humble and grateful efforts. This is the devotional or emotional side of Hinduism. The Hinduand as a rationalist, perceives God, as the All-pervading Supreme Intelligence, and as the All-pervading Supreme Spiritual Essence—in short, as the one *Para-Brahma* or *Paramâtmâ*. The Hindu, as a devotionalist, realizes the presence of the All-loving and the gracious Supreme One—in short, the *Satchitânanda*.

Thus Hindu philosophy and the Hindu religion proper meet, though proceeding from different stand-points. Bodhsara says:—

"The one class (the emotionalists) worship God saying, 'I am Thine'; the other (the rationalists) worship him, saying, 'I am not different from Thee'. Though they differ a little the result is the same".*

The character of the two Revelations, is illustrated by an examination of the operation of the external senses of man. Take for instance, the sense of sight. It has, like every other sense, two aspects—a dry perceptive aspect and the sweet emotional aspect. In the perceptive aspect of sight, a knowledge of existence, is all that is produced. In its emotional aspect it brings home the impression of beauty. Thus the perceptive phase of vision, which corresponds with rationalism, relates to the dry and general question of existence. But the other phase of it, con-

---

* तवास्मीति भजन्त्वेके त्वमेवास्मीति चापरे
इति किञ्चिद्विशेषेऽपि परिणामः समोद्वयोः ।

Bodhsara (Bh. Y. 6.)

sisting of the realization of beauty, corresponds with emotionalism. It is so with all the external senses of man. His highest sense, therefore, the object of which is spiritual, has also the same double aspect, namely, the rational aspect and the emotional aspect.

Sir Issac Newton, in discovering laws after laws in physics and mathematics, widened the rationalistic view of the student of Nature. But when he exclaimed that his discoveries were but an atom in the supreme design and scheme of the Universe, his heart felt just the same sort of emotion which moved Milton in putting in the mouth of the first man, the well-known prayer, "These are thy glorious works, Parent of good, Almighty, &c."

The sciences generally embody the results of the study of Nature, from a rationalistic point of view. Each science, within its limits, proves the existence of order and law. As they rise in their scale, or become wider in their scope, they tend to demonstrate Supreme Intelligence ruling everywhere and in all things. That science, which we have called the science of religion, as contained in the *Jnāna Kānda* of Hinduism, shows in full, what other sciences tend to, *viz*, that everything is ultimately resolvable into an All-pervading Intelligence and an All-powerful Supreme Will. Thus it may be said that, even the natural sciences such as, Astronomy, Physiology, Botany, Chemistry, Physics, and the rest, all lead up to the science of Religion, which therefore may be called the crowning science.

But if Vedantism is the crowning science, the religion of *Nishkāma Prema* (*i. e.* the religion of disinterested Love) is the crowning art of all arts. All material arts further the happiness of man, and inspire in him grateful feelings. The fine arts chasten and elevate him, for, who can deny that when properly directed, music, painting, sculpture, and poetry all exalt and purify man. In fact, all the arts of human life, when fitly appreciated, verify the goodness of Providence. The large the number of the higher arts you cultivate, the loftier and wider is the field of Divine goodness and love presented to you. It is thus the higher arts gradually tend to develop the religion of disinterested love towards God and when he feels such love towards Him, he begins to resort to the tactics of a lover which may be called the art of *Nishkāma Prema*, the highest of all arts. Thus while Vedantism reveals God as *Para-Brahma*, *Prem-Bhakti* reveals Him as Sri Krishna.

Section 4—Hinduism combines the two Revelations.

As stated before Hinduism combines the Revelations of Rationalism and Emotionalism, in other words, it combines the Revelations of spiritual science and of spiritual art.

"As the two wings of a bird ensure its motion so do *Jnana* and *Karma* lead to the attainment of beatitude."*

उभाभ्यामेव पक्षाभ्यां यथा खे पक्षिणां गतिः।
तथैव ज्ञान कर्म्माभ्यां जायते परमं पदम् ॥

Yoga Vashista Ramayana (1-1-7).

The spiritual science which is the highest of all sciences comes through the most comprehensive, purified and discriminating inspired sense of the Rishis and saints. The spiritual art which is the highest of all arts is developed by the most self-sacrificing devotion and love of the *Bhaktas*.

The *Jnana Kânda* of the Vedas, corresponds to the *Jnana Yoga* of *Srimat Bhagabat Geeta*, and to the principles of philosophy known as Vedântism.

The *Karma Kânda* of the Vedas, corresponds to the *Karma Yoga* or *Bhakti Yoga* of *Geeta*, and to those principles of *Bhakti* known as *Purânism*.

Thus at every stage and in every form of the sacred scriptures of the Hindus, Rationalism is combined with Emotionalism; in other words, the Revelation of spiritual science is combined with the Revelation of spiritual art.

"Shâstras know no difference between rationalists and emotionalists."*

---

* न भक्तज्ञानिनोर्दृष्टा शास्त्रे लक्षणभिन्नता।

Bodhasar Bhakti Yoga (3)

The revelation of *Jnana* is wedded to the Revelation of *Bhakti* and *Karma*, as thought is wedded to fact; or as ideas are wedded to words. Should one seek to divorce them, he would be seeking to mar both of them.

If one, full of rationalism, should wish to dispense with emotionalism, he would be in the same position as one who, being versed in the science of music, denies himself the sweetness of a song, which is the art of music; or as one who, being versed in the science of electricity, shuts himself out from the conveniences and comforts, derived from the telegraph or such other electric arts.

The bond of union between them is broken, when they are perverted from their true character, for instance, when the *Jnana Kânda* is allowed to degenerate into scepticism or sophism, and to *Karma Kânda* is suffered to lapse into sensual superstition or mere ritualism.

But so long as the *Jnana Kânda* is cultivated as a true spiritual science, it keeps its basis as the highest of all sciences, and stands above sophism or materialism; so also so long the *Bhakti Kânda* is earnestly practised, it maintains its position as the highest of all arts,—the art of salvation,—free from all taints of superstition or dead ritualism. Of the two, however, the average man may rather dispense with the *Jnana Kânda*, than the *Karma* and *Bhakti Kândas*, just as the average man may rather dispense with the sciences, than the common arts of life.

It should be noticed here that in Hindu books, the word *Jnana* is sometimes used in an extended sense, meaning not only rationalism but also emotionalism *i. e.* as including both *Viveka* and *Bhakti.**

The word *Karma*, on the other hand, is often used in a limited sense, as denoting only acts done, rather mechanically, than as the manifestation of *Bhakti*.

---

* श्रवणं मननञ्चैव ध्यानं भक्तिस्तथैव च ।
न चैतानि विना कश्चित् ज्ञानमाप कुतश्चन ॥

Naradiya.

तेषां ज्ञानी नित्ययुक्त एकभक्तिर्विशिष्यते ।

Geeta (7-17)

When the terms are used in the above sense, of course, *Jnana* becomes the highest stage of spiritual development, in a harmonized form, to which *Karma* stands only as something low down in the scale.

Jnana in this extended sense, is not only a dry knowledge of the Deity, but a feeling realization of His loving presence.*

In any healthy system of Religion and Ethics, the principles of Rationalism and Emotionalism must be, more or less, combined. The main spring of Rationalism of the Hindus is the Upanishads. But the Upanishads, far from repudiating the principles of Emotionalism, distinctly sanction them. Even the Darshans, not excepting the Shankhya, directly or indirectly support and vindicate those cardinal principles of Emotionalism which underlie the worship of the

---

* संदृश्यते वाप्यधिगम्यते वा
तज्ज्ञानमज्ञानमतोऽन्यदुक्तम् ।

Bishnu Purana (6-5-87).

तद्विज्ञानेन परिपश्यन्ति धीरा-
आनन्दरूपममृतं यद्विभाति ॥

Mundaka Upanishad (2-2-7).

Deity as a Personality in various shapes, such as *Srimurti* and *Jugal-murti* (the Divine personality in a single or dual shape.)

Section 5.—The same subject : The Upanishads and Darshanas.

The Chhandogya Upanishad is one of the extremely abstract Upanishads in which the well-known and oft-quoted passage '*Tattwamasi*' occurs. Even the Chhandogya lays dawn :—

"This whole universe is in God. Every thing proceeds from Him, ends in Him, and rests in Him. Composing oneself, one should worship Him. Purusha is made of action, as he acts so he enjoys or suffers. Therefore he must perform religious duties."* This shows that the phrase '*Tattwamasi*'

---

* सर्व्वं खल्विदं ब्रह्म तज्जलानिति शान्त उपासीत अथ खलु क्रतुमयः पुरुषो यथाक्रतुरस्मिँल्लोँके पुरुषो भवति तथेतः प्रेत्य भवति स क्रतुं कुर्वीत ।

Chhandogya Upanishad (3-14-1).

means 'thou livest in God and hast occult divine power, capable of unlimited development by devotion.'

Then in Kena Upanishad is the following :—

"That God is to be worshipped by all, and as He is to be worshipped, it is necessary to pray to Him. The man, who knows Him thus, becomes the object of regard to all."*

Again, Swetaswatara Upanishad, has the following :—

"As by pressing, you get oil out of the oil-seed, as by churning the curdled milk, you get butter, as by digging in the dry bed of a river, you get water, as by rubbing the *Aravi* wood you get fire, so by earnest seeking, with truth and self-sacrifice, you find the Supreme Deity even in your own heart."†

It is not necessary to multiply instances

---

* तद्ध तद्वनं नाम तद्वनमित्युपासितव्यं स य एतदेवं वेदाऽभि हैनं सर्वाणि भूतानि संवाञ्छन्ति ।

Sloka—6. -Kanda—4.

† तिलेषु तैलं दधिनीव सर्पिराप स्रोतःस्वरणीषु चाग्निः ।
एवमात्मात्मनि गृह्यतेऽसौ सत्येनैनं तपसा योऽनुपश्यति ॥

Verse—15. Chap. I.

from the Upanishads, enjoining worship and prayer. The Upanishads are, in fact, supplementary to the *Karma Kânda*. The Bodhasâr puts the difference between the *Jnani* and *Bhakta* as follows :—

"To the *Jnani* salvation is the chief aim, *Bhakti* is its means. To the *Bhakta* reverential love is his chief aim, and salvation is its concomitant."*

The Vedanta Darshana also confirms and establishes the principles of *Bhakti* and *Karma*—devotion and worship. Numerous sects of Yogis and Sanyasis have sprung up who read the Vedanta Darshana and other Hindu Scriptures in a very strange way, and maintain, that renunciation, not only of all works, but of all forms of worship and devotion, is the highest stage of Hinduism, and that *Bhakti* and *Karma i. e.* acts of worship and prayer as well as reverence, are things inferior and are only valuable as constituting the steps to *Sanyas* and *Bairâgya*.

It has been already seen that the Upani-

---

* मुक्तिर्मुख्यफलं ज्ञस्य भक्तिस्तत्साधनत्वतः ।
भक्तस्य भक्तिर्मुख्या स्यान्मुक्तिः स्यादानुसङ्गिकी ॥

shads inculcate *Sâdhana* and *Karma*, as things of primary importance. In this respect the Vedanta Darshana, so differently understood, is by no means behind. One distinct part of it is devoted to *Sâdhana.* It declares that the Rational and the Emotional methods (*Jnana* and *Karma*) are both equally sanctioned.*

"The personal form of God, being described by imagery."†

"His manifestability is unfailing."‡

However differently these *sutras* may be interpreted, there can be but little doubt, that there is not much difference between the meaning of the aforesaid *sutras* and the following well-known *sloka* of the Bhagabat Geeta.

"However men approach Me, even so do

---

* तुल्यन्तु दर्शनम् ।

Vedanta Sutra—9. Sec—4. Chap. III.

† रूपोपन्यासाच्च ।

Vedanta Sutra—23. Sec—2. Chap. I.

‡ प्रकाशवच्चावैयर्थ्यात् ।

Vedanta Sutra—15. Sec—2. Chap. III.

I accept them, for the path men take from every side is mine, O Partha." *

The Uttar Geeta formulates the following question :—

"There can be no contemplation of what is not visible. The visible again is perishable. How to fix then attention upon formless God. The conditioned personal form, is open to the objection of transiency, the unconditioned impersonal form, again is open to the objection of blankness. If, then, both are objectionable how to fix attention on Him."†

The following from Bishnu-Purana is an answer to the above question of Uttar Geeta :—

---

* ये यथा मां प्रपद्यन्ते तांस्तथैव भजाम्यहम् ।
मम वर्त्मानुवर्त्तन्ते मनुष्याः पार्थ सर्वशः ॥

(4-11)

† अदृश्ये भावना नास्ति दृश्यमेतद्विनश्यति ।
अवर्णमीश्वरं ब्रह्म कथं ध्यायन्ति योगिनः ।
सालम्बस्याप्यनित्यत्वं निरालम्बस्य शून्यता ।
उभयोरपि दोषित्वात् कथं ध्यायन्ति योगिनः ।

Uttar Geeta (1-35 & 37)

"God is both Individualized and Universalized, both Manifest and Unmanifest."*

The Panchadasi also solves the difficulty.

"Although He is unknowable, He is perceived by the devotee and hence He is called—Self-manifesting."†

Again in the Sruti already quoted it is found: "Brahma is to be known in a two-fold form, the *Para* and the *Apara*."

Thus the quarrel between the Adwaitabadis *i. e.* those who assert the perfection of the Deity form an impersonal point of view, and the Dwaitabadis *i. e.* those who worship Him as a perfect personality, is futile.‡ In fact, the conception of His Impersonal perfection, only sets off His Personality, as

---

* स ईश्वरो व्यष्टिसमष्टिरूपो
व्यक्तस्वरूपोऽप्रकटस्वरूपः ॥

(6-5-85)

† अवेद्योऽप्यापरोक्षोऽतः स्वप्रकाशो भवत्ययम् ।

(3-28)

‡ अद्वैतं केचिदिच्छन्ति द्वैतमिच्छन्ति चापरे ।
मम तत्त्वं न जानन्ति द्वैताद्वैतविवर्ज्जितम् ॥

Kularnava Tantra (5-1-110).

the Upanishads show. To the heart and reason the Almighty responds, as personal, though infinite. To the bare intellect, He sometimes appears as impersonal. God is, thus, personal and at the same time more or less impersonal. The evidence of the heart, is certainly, no less weighty than that of the intellect. They are moreover not inconsistent with each other. 'The Supreme Soul as Truth, Intelligence and Bliss' (सत्यम् ज्ञानम् आनन्दम्) cannot be different from the Supreme Person as full of Truth, Intelligence and Bliss (सत् चित् आनन्द). Yet this is all the difference between the two *badas*, *i. e.* dogmas.

CHAPTER IV.

Illustrative Texts of the two Revelations from the Vedas.

Section 1.—Illustrative Text of Jnana Kanda and Karma Kanda from the Kausitaki Upanishad and 28th Sukta, 1st Mandal, Rigveda.

The Hindu Scriptures recognize Devata (divinity) in the sun, the moon and the planets and of the various principles of physical energy, such as the liquifying principle, the heating principle, the ethereal principle, &c. There are hymns in the Vedas addressed severally to these *Devatas*. In Chapter IV of the Kausitaki Upanishad of the Rigveda, a discussion is held as to how these hymns are really to be understood.

Balaki, of the family of Garga, maintains that, these hymns are prayers offered to the several presiding spirits or Devatas as indicated by the name of the object over which he presides.

Ajat Satru, on the other hand, maintains that, the prayers are intended to mean a thankful recognition of the several beneficial and wonderful qualities, which these objects —the sun, the moon, the liquifying principle, and the heat-generating principle, &c.— respectively possess.

Apparently Ajat Satru is arguing, as a materialist or positivist of the present day would do. But really he is far from such a line of argument. He says that the sun, the moon and other things are all created objects. Man ought to know and worship the Supreme Being, who created them. Thus, when he says he worships the sun, the moon and other things, because of their qualities, he really says that he worships them as manifesting the goodness and beneficence of the Supreme Being.

Thus this Upanishad reveals the Supreme Being as the Infinite one, who dispenses all that is good and that gives power to man. This Revelation is rational because it proceeds from reasoning and inference.

The following is an extract* of the passage in the Kausitaki Upanishad referred to above.

Says Garga Balaki. "The person in the sun is worshipped by me."

---

* स होवाच वालाकिर्य एवैष आदित्ये पुरुषस्तमेवाहमुपास इति तं होवाचाजातशत्रुर्मा मैतस्मिन् संवादयिष्ठा बृहत्पाण्डुरवासा अतिष्ठाः सर्वेषां भूतानां मूर्द्धेति वा अहमेतमुपास इति स यो हैतमेवमुपास्तेऽतिष्ठाः सर्वेषां भूतानां मूर्द्धा भवति । ३ ।

स होवाच वालाकिर्य एवैष चन्द्रमसि पुरुषस्तमेवाहमुपास इति तं होबाचाजातशत्रुर्मा मैतस्मिन् संवादयिष्ठा अन्नस्यात्मेति वा अहमेतमुपास इति स यो हैतमेवमुपास्तेऽन्नस्यात्मा भवति ॥ ४ ॥

स होवाच वालाकिर्य एवैष विद्युति पुरुषस्तमेवाहमुपास इति तं होवाचाजातशत्रुर्मा मैतस्मिन् संवादयिष्ठाः सत्यस्यात्मेति वा अहमेतमुपास इति स यो हैतमेवमुपास्ते सत्यस्यात्मा भवति । ५ ।

तत उ ह वालाकिस्तूष्णीमास तं होवाचाजातशत्रुरेतावन्नु वालाका इत्येतावदिति होवाच बालाकिस्तं होवाचाजातशत्रु मृषा वै खलु मा संवादयिष्ठा ब्रह्म ते ब्रवाणीति यो वै वालाक एतेषां पुरुषाणां कर्त्ता यस्य वै तत्कर्म स वै वेदितव्य इति ॥ १९ ॥

Says Ajatsatru.—"Don't you make me contradict you on this point. The sun is worshipped by me because he is bright, unchangeable and the fountain-head of all beings. He who worships the sun in this way becomes superior to all."

Says Balaki,—"The person in the moon is worshipped by me,"

Says Ajatsatru.—"Don't you make me contradict you on this point. The moon is worshipped by me because he is the soul of all that sustains life. He that worship the moon in this way becomes the lord of food."

Says Balaki.—"The person in the Lightning is worshipped by me."

Says Ajatsatru.—"Don't you make me contradict you on this point. The Lightning is worshipped by me because he is the soul of rains. He that worships Lightning becomes cool-hearted."

After this Balaki became silent. Ajatsatru said to him: "Balaki! This is the limit of your *Jnana* (knowledge)." Balaki said, "yes". Ajatsatru said, "I have, led by you, contradicted your assertions so long, because I want to tell you in detail of the Supreme Being, Oh Balaki !"

"He who is the Creator of the sun, the moon &c. by whom the sun, the moon, &c. have been created, is the One whom we ought to know."

Later on, Ajatsatru explains, by referring to the phenomenon of human existence that, as in the case of man, the whole body is animated by that spark of consciousness, called the soul, which gives vitality to each part of the body without being traceable to any particular part of it, so does the Great Spirit of the Universe animate whole Nature without being identifiable with any part of it.

Thus this Upanishad reveals the Supreme Being as the Infinite one who dispenses all that is good and who provides all that gives power to man. This Revelation is rational.

The following is an instance of *Bhakti Kânda* or Emotional Revelation:

The devotee, feeling the presence of God in his own heart, looks around to see Him in the external world. He finds Him there, as the one already known to him, and dear to him. He is propelled to welcome Him, to make offerings to Him and to sing His praise. But he hardly knows by what name to call Him, and how to describe Him. Now he calls Him by one name and now by another. Now he describes Him in one way and now in another.

In the following hymn of the Rigveda, (1st *Mandal*, 28th *Sukta*), the votary calls Him Varuna, and figures Him as the overshadowing genius of the Creation, and thus outpours his heart to Him.

1. "Come ye—the all-skilful and self-radiant Varuna—whose another name is Aditya—come and partake of this offering. He overpowers the whole Nature by His glory. The radiant Lord Varuna cheers His worshippers. I desire to praise Him."

2. "May we, O Lord! Contemplate and praise and serve Thee as we ought, and thus deserve success."

"May we daily, just as the Aurora breaks in with rays of light, brighten ourselves by praising Thee."

3. "Thou Leader of the world, Thou hast legions of heroes to follow, multitudes to

parise Thee; may we find a corner in Thine great house to take shelter in."

"Ye—the envyless bright children of the Infinite—do you forgive our sins as friends of us."

4. "Varuna, the son of the Infinite, the upholder of the world, brought water into existence in a wonderful manner. By His glory the rivers run and never rest nor pause. They run as swift as the birds in the skies."

5. "O Varuna, my sins have bound me up as by a rope—do Thou let me loose from them. May we reach Thy river full of divine water. May not our *Yagna* (act of sacrifice) break when put to its strain, may not its measure untimely fail."

6. "O Varuna, free us from fear; Thou Highest King and Highest Truth, be gracious unto us. Free us from the bondage of sin as a calf is freed from its tying string, for severed from Thee, none can exert influence for a second."

7. "Thou Hero, Varuna, destructive are the weapons of vengeance that overtake those who fail in ihe performance of sacrifice unto Thee. May we give no occasion for such

weapons. May we not be banished from light. Let the mischievous be confounded so that our lives may be saved."

8. "Thou manifested in various places, may the words 'we bow down to Thee' be uttered in the past, present and the future—as unto Thee, gracious Varuna, all good deeds of men go forth and remain entwined as around a mountain."

9. "O Varuna, let the debts of our ancestors as well as of ourselves be discharged by Thee. May I not be compelled to enjoy wealth acquired by others. May we be permitted to live a real life during the many mornings (*Ushas*) that may yet come."

10. "Thou Sovereign, I am timid—protect me against fear inspired by friends, relatives or fancies. May my life be saved from the attempt of thieves or animals."

11. "Thou Varuna, may I not be subjected to the humiliation of serving the rich or the generous from the poverty of my kith and kin. We, sons and grand-sons, together sing hymns at this sacrifice.

Section 2.—The Same Subject continued : Kena Upanishad and 55th Sukta, 3rd Mandal, Rigveda.

The Kausitaki Upanishad teaches that, one should worship the wonderful, beautiful and blissful phenomena of Nature, more as manifestations of the supreme goodness, and supreme intelligence of Almighty God, rather than as the manifestations of the individual *Devatas*, or the spirits who might severally preside over them piecemeal. The Kena Upanishad of the Sama Veda teaches the same thing. But first of all it declares the omnipotence and the omniscience of God as follows :—*

1. Pupil—"By whom directed, mind pursues its objects ? By whom is life first set to move on? By whom wished, are words

* ओं केनेषितं पतति प्रेषितं मनः केन प्राणः प्रथमः प्रैति युक्तः। केनेषितां वाचमिमां वदन्ति चक्षुः श्रोत्रं क उ देवो युनक्ति ॥ १ ॥

श्रोत्रस्य श्रोत्रं मनसो मनो यद्वाचो ह वाचं स उ प्राणस्य प्राणश्चक्षुषश्चक्षुरतिमुच्य धीराः प्रेत्यास्माल्लोकादमृता भवन्ति ॥ २ ॥

uttered? By whom are eyes and ears each directed to their functions?"

2. Teacher—"He is the ear of the ear, mind of the mind, word of the word, life of the life, and eye of the eye. When wise men know Him as such they give up worldly desires and leaving the mortal world become immortal,"

Then it goes on to illustrate by a parable that the power of every *Devata* is derived from the Supreme Being.

The following lines are taken from the parable :—*

5. "After this, God asked Fire-god—'What heroism dost thou possess?' Answered Fire-god—"I can burn everything in this world."

6. "God placed a straw before Fire and said, 'Burn this.' Fire set himself with all

---

* तस्मिंस्त्वयि किं वीर्यमित्यपीदं सर्वं दहेयं यदिदं पृथिव्यामिति ॥ ५ ॥

तस्मै तृणं निदधावेतद्दहेति तदुपप्रेयाय सर्वजवेन तन्न शशाक दग्धुं स तत एव निववृते नैतदशकं विज्ञातुं यदेतद् यक्षमिति ॥ ६ ॥

his force at the straw, but could not burn it. Returning baffled he said, 'who is this God, I am anxious to know.' "

"9. After this God asked Air-god, 'What heroism dost thou posses?' Answered Air-god, 'I can take in everthing in the world.' "

"10. God placed a straw before Air and said, 'Take this in.' Air set himself at this straw with all his force, but could not take it in. Returning baffled he said 'Who this God is, I am anxious to knwo.

This is Revelation of a rational kind. But the same truth is brought home forcibly and vividly by devotion and emotionalism.

See the following lines from a certain hymn on a kindred subject. *(55th Sukta, 3rd Mandal,* Rigveda).*

तस्मिंस्त्वयि किं वीर्य्यमित्यपीदं सर्वमाददीयं यदिदं पृथिव्यामिति ॥ ९ ॥

तस्मै तृणं निदधावेतदादत्स्वेति तदुपप्रेयाय सर्व-जवेन तन्न शशाकादातुं स तत एव निववृते नैतदशकं विज्ञातुं यदेतद् यक्षमिति ॥ १० ॥

* माता च यत्र दुहिता च धेनू
सबर्दुघे धापयेते समीची ।

"12. I sing the praise of the Two, the Genius of Earth and the Genious of Firmament. who like Mother and Daughter meet in the space between, and entertain each other with nectarean fluids, is the midst of the regions where rains gather. Both of you derive your great power from the same source."

"13 The one (Firmament) licking the offspring—the other (Eerth)—makes a sound and soaks all the moisture of the earth to wet his upper regions, but the earth again gets water from the lord of the heavens. Thus the power of both is derived from the same source"

"19 He (Twasta) who sends forth all

ऋतस्य ते सदसीले अंतर्मह-
द्देवानामसुरत्वमेकं ॥ १२ ॥
अन्यस्या वत्सं रिहती मिमाय
कया भुवा निदधे धेनुरूधः ।
ऋतस्य सा पयसापिन्वतेला
महद्देवानामसुरत्वमेकं ॥ १३ ॥
देवस्त्वष्टा सविता विश्वरूपः
पुपोष प्रजाः पुरुधा जजान ।

things and creatures, assume different forms and in various ways causes offsprings to be born and maintained The power of the Devatas is derived from the same source."

"20. He has adorned the Firmament and the Earth with birds and quadrupeds. Both of them are imbued with the stamina of the same Indra. He is powerful and deprives bad men of their resources. The power of the Devatas is derived from the same source."

"21. He is the supporter of the universe and our King, is between the Earth and the Firmament as the benefactor of all. The Hero moves before Indra and lives in

---

इमा च विश्वा भुवनान्यस्य
महद्देवानामसुरत्वमेकं ॥ १९ ॥
मही समैरच्चम्वा समीची
उभे ते अस्य वसुना न्यृष्ट ।
आखे वीरो विंदमानो वसूनि
महद्देवानामसुरत्वमेकम् ॥ २० ॥
इमां च नः पृथिवीं विश्वधाया
उपक्षेति हितमित्रो न राजा ।

his house. The power of the Devatas is derived from the same source."

Section 3.—The Same Subject Continued: Katha Upanishad and 89th Sukta, 7th Mandal, Rigveda.

The Katha Upanishad of the Krishna Yayurveda teaches how the soul of man is immortal and spiritual, and how man, by giving up selfish desires and by indulging in the disinterested discharge of duty, is purified and saved.*

"1. The thing 'Sreyas' (sense of duty) is different from the thing 'preyas' (sense of pleasure). Men are influenced by them for

---

पुरः सदः शर्म्मसदो न वीरा
मह्द्देवानामसुरत्वमेकं ॥ २१ ॥

* अन्यच्छ्रेयोऽन्यदुतैव प्रेयस्ते
उभे नानार्थे पुरुषं सिनीतः ।
तयोः श्रेय आददानस्य साधु भवति
हीयतेऽर्थाद् य उ प्रेयो वृणीते ॥ १ ॥

different purposes. He who follows the sense of pleasure, is deprived of the supreme purpose of life. He who follows the sense of duty is blessed in his life."

"2. The sense of duty and the sense of pleasure take hold of all men. The calm reflecting man separates the one from the other. The wise gives preference to the sense of duty to that of pleasure tending to bodily comforts."

"3. Natchiketa ! You have eschewed pleasurable, enticing and charming things. You have not accepted expectations heaped together of worldly resources in which men sink."

श्रेयश्च प्रेयश्च मनुष्यमेतस्तौ
सम्परीत्य विविनक्ति धीरः ।
श्रेयो हि धीरोऽभिप्रेयसो वृणीते
प्रेयो मन्दो योगक्षेमाद्वृणीते ॥ २ ॥
स त्वं प्रियान् प्रियरूपांश्च कामा-
नभिध्यायन्नचिकेतोऽत्यस्राक्षीः ।
नैतां सृङ्कां वित्तमयीमवाप्तो
यस्यां मज्जन्ति बहवो मनुष्याः ॥ ३ ॥
दूरमेते विपरीते विषुची
अविद्या या च विद्येति ज्ञाता ।

"4. True realization (*Vidya*) and false realization (*Avidya*) are opposite to each other, and have different courses. I know Natchiketa, you are devoted to true realization, for many a tempting thing has failed to shake you from your resolution to stick to the sense of duty."

"15. The Being of whom all the Vedas sing, for whom all penances are gone through, for attaining whom, men perform *Brahmacharya*, that Being briefly speaking is indicated by the syllable *Om.*"

"16. This indestructible is Brahma, this indestructible is ParaBrahma. Whoever wishes for a thing in view of this Indestructible, that thing becomes surely his."

विद्याभीप्सिनन्नचिकेतसं मन्ये

न त्वा कामा बहवेा लोलुपन्त ॥ ४ ॥

सर्वे वेदा यत्पदमामनन्ति

तपांसि सर्वाणि च यद्वदन्ति ।

यदिच्छन्तेा ब्रह्मचर्य्यञ्चरन्ति

तत्ते पदं सङ्ग्रहेण ब्रवीम्योमित्येतत् ॥ १५ ॥

एतद्धोग्रवाक्षरं ब्रह्म एतदेवाक्षरम्परम् ।

एतद्धोंवाक्षरं ज्ञात्वा यो यदिच्छति तस्य तत् ॥ १६ ॥

"17. This is the best aim, this is the highest aim. He who knows this aim acquires greatness in the highest heavens—*Brahmaloka.*"

The above is a rational exposition of the importance of purifying life by giving up selfishness and by making a sacrifice of self. Purification of life, by rising over selfishness, is more effectively secured by prayer and devotion, *i. e.*—emotionalism. In the Rigveda, prayers for self-purification abound. The following short hymn *(Sukta 89, 7th Mandal,* Rigveda) addressed to Varuna will illustrate the emotional process of purifying and strengthening the mind.*

"1. Thou Lord Varuna! May I not be doomed to the earthly habitation. Be kind, Almighty, be kind.

"2. Thou all-powerful, I am drifted

एतदालम्बनं श्रेष्ठमेतदालम्बनम्परम् ।
एतदालम्बनं ज्ञात्वा ब्रह्मलोके महीयते ॥ १७ ॥

* मो षु वरुण मृन्मयं गृहं राजन्नहं गमं । मृला सुक्षत्र मृलय ॥ १ ॥

यदेमि प्रस्फुरन्निव दृतिर्न ध्मातो अद्रिवः । मृला सुक्षत्र मृलय ॥ २ ॥

as a cloud by the wind, trembling and trepidating. Be kind, Almighty, be kind."

"3. Thou master of wealth, I am reduced to adversity through weakness. Be kind, Almighty, be kind."

"4. Thy adorer gets thirsty, even living in water. Be kind, Almighty, be kind,"

"5. Be pleased not to punish us for we may have done against Divine Beings (*Devatas*) and for neglecting your works,—for we are weak men, Oh Varuna."

क्रत्वः समह दीनता प्रतीपं जगमा शुचे। मृला सुक्षत्र मृलय ॥ ३ ॥

अपां मध्ये तस्थिवांसं तृष्णाविदज्जरितारम्। मृला सुक्षत्र मृलय ॥ ४ ॥

यत् किं चेदं वरुण दैव्ये जनेऽभिद्रोहं मनुष्याश्चरामसि। अचित्ती यत्तव धर्मा युयोपिम मा नस्तस्मादेनसो देव रीरिषः ॥ ५ ॥

Section 4.—The Same Subject continued : Isha Upanishad and 7th Sukta, 1st Mundal, Rigveda.

The Isha Upanishad of the Shukla Yayurveda, lays down the high truths revealed by reason regarding the Supreme Being, and the destinies of man in the following terms* :—

"1. God pervades all this, that goes by the name of Universe. Enjoy all this without any attachment *i. e.* without the sense, that this is your own ; for that is the source of misery. Do not covet what belongs to others."

"2. In this field of work, desire to live the longest period allowed, working and for work. This is the law for you, and not otherwise. Work does not stick to man."

"3. Those men, who by way of committing suicide are averse to secure salvation of

---

* ईशा वास्यमिदं सर्वं यत् किञ्च जगत्याञ्जगत् ।
तेन त्यक्तेन भुञ्जीथा मा गृधः कस्य स्विद्धनम् ॥ १ ॥
कुर्वन्नेवेह कर्म्माणि जिजीविषेच्छतं समाः ।
एवं त्वयि नान्यथेतोऽस्ति न कर्म्म लिप्यते नरे ॥ २ ॥

self, go to a world known as the sunless dark world."

"4. That Supreme Being is without a second, He is unmoving, but at the same time moves faster than mind. *Devatas* all lag behind Him. Although He is stationary, yet He is pursuing, and out-strips all. The moving elements, water and air, are all in His embrace."

"5. He goes everywhere, although He is motionless; He is far, though near; He is in the innermost recesses of everything, at the same time He is around everything."

असुर्य्या नाम ते लोका अन्धेन तमसावृता: ।
तांस्ते प्रेत्याभिगच्छन्ति ये के चात्महनो जना: ॥ ३ ॥

Isha Upanishad. Chap XL.

अनेजदेकम्मनसो जवीयो
नैनद्देवा आप्नुवन् पूर्बमर्षत् ।
तद्धावतोऽन्यानत्येति तिष्ठत्त·
स्मिन्नपो मातरिश्वा दधाति ॥ ४ ॥

तदेजति तन्नैजति तद्दूरे तद्वदन्तिके ।
तदन्तरस्य सर्वस्य तदु सर्वस्याश्य वाह्यत: ॥ ५ ॥

"9. Those who pay homage to ignorance enter dark regions. Those again who are addicted to knowledge, enter regions yet darker."

"10. Knowledge bears a particular fruit, and so also ignorance. This is a common saying, and we have heard the same from wise men, who have instructed us in the subject."

"11. He, who simultaneously masters both knowledge and ignorance, escapes from death by ignorance and attains to immortality by knowledge."

"12. Those who pay homage to a want of faith in causâlity, enter the darkmost

---

अन्धन्तमः प्रविशन्ति येऽविद्यामुपासते ।
ततो भूय इव ते तमो य उ विद्यायां रताः ॥ ९ ॥
अन्यदेवाहुर्बिद्ययान्यदेबाहुरविद्यया ।
इति शुश्रुम धीराणां ये नस्तद्विचचक्षिरे ॥ १० ॥
विद्याञ्चाविद्याञ्च यस्तद्वेदोभयं सह ।
अविद्यया मृत्युन्तीर्त्वा विद्ययाऽमृतमश्नुते ॥ ११ ॥
अन्धन्तमः प्रविशन्ति येऽसम्भूतिमुपासते !
ततो भूय इव ते तमो य उ सम्भूत्यां रताः ॥ १२ ॥

regions. Those again, who are addicted to seeking causality, enter yet darker regions."

"13. The one bears one particular fruit and the other bears another particular fruit. This is a common saying. We have heard the same from wise men, who have instructed us in the same subject."

"14. He, who simultaneously masters both the principle of causation and destruction, escapes from death by his sense of destruction and attains to immortality by his sense of causation."

The truths, stated above, are all grand and high. But nevertheless, being expressed in the dry light of reason, there is not that flesh and blood about them, which are found in utterances inspired by devotion and reverence, *i. e.*, emotionalism. The following hymn addressed to Indra *(7th Sukta. 1st Mundal*, Rigveda) shows how the worship

---

अन्यदेवाहुः सम्भवादन्यदाहुरसम्भवात् ।
इति शुश्रुम धीराणां ये नस्तद्विचचक्षिरे ॥ १३ ॥
सम्भूतिञ्च विनाशञ्च यस्तद्वेदोभयं सह ।
विनाशेन मृत्युन्तीर्त्वा सम्भूत्यामृतमश्नुते ॥ १४ ॥

of God idealized or localized in the worshipper's own way, under the name Indra, tends to give that pure comfort and relief and that strong assurance which many a dry text is incapable of giving.

1. Indra is worshipped with songs by the singers, with hymns by those who can recite hymns, with garlands of epithets by others.

2. Indra visits all, instantly yoking his two *haries*. He is powerful and glorious.

3. He has placed the sun in the sky, to have a distant view of things, and the sun by his rays illuminates the mountains.

4. Potent Lord! protect us in our worship and our thousand great battles by your unfailing guardiantly care.

5. Indra is our help and bears arms against those who do us evil. We invoke his aid for great as well as small things.

6. Thou giver of all fruits of action, thou giver of rains, mayest thou break these clouds into showers. Thou art never disappointing.

7. The best hymns addressed to different *Devatas* adored for different pur-

poses, go to the service of Indra, the bearer of Indra, the bearer of thunder. I know not properly to sing his praise.

8. As the way towards the forest fills the bullocks with strength, so does Indra ever showering what man desires, fills men with strength. He is as powerful as willing to grant prayers.

9. He is Indra who above reigns over all men, all things and the five *Kshitis.*

10. Who is above all people, Him I invoke for the sake of you all, may He be ours only.

SECTION 5—THE SAME SUBJECT CONTINUED. THE BRIHAT ARANYAKA UPANISHAD AND 12TH SUKTA, 2nd MANDAL, RIGVEDA.

THE Brihat Aranyaka Upanishad of the Shukla Yajurveda gives instructions as to how the transcendental spirituality and unity of the God-head are conceived, (3rd Chapter, 8th Brahmana, Slokas 7 to 9.)*

* स होवाच यदूर्ध्वं गार्गि दिवो यदवाक् पृथिव्या यदन्तरा द्यावापृथिवी इमे यद्भूतञ्च भवच्च भविष्यच्चेत्याचक्षत

"7. Yajnavalka said—Gargi! That pervading thing which exists above the heavens, below the earth, in the regions between, that which is known as existing in past and in the future, is *Akâsa* or ether. Gargi asked, "what is the substratum of that *Akâsa* or ether?"

"8. Says Yajnavalkya—Gargi! He is the *Akshara*. Those who have known Brahma, say,—He is neither gross nor fine, neither short nor long, neither burning like fire nor dissolving like water. He is not shadowy and confused. He is neither the air, nor the ether. He does not require eyes, ears, nor organs of speech, nor the mind for perception and sensation. For His existence neither the vital heat nor the vital air are necessary, &c., &c.

आकाश एव तदोतञ्च प्रोतञ्चेति कस्मिन्नु खल्वाकाश ओतश्च प्रोतश्चेति ॥ ७ ॥

स होवाचैतद्वै तदक्षरं गार्गि ब्राह्मणा अभिवदन्त्यस्थूलमनण्वह्रस्वमदीर्घमलोहितमस्नेहमच्छायमतोऽवाय्वनाकाशमसङ्गमरसमगन्धमचक्षुष्कमश्रोत्रमवागमनोऽतेजस्कमप्राणममुखममात्रमनन्तरमवाह्यं न तदश्नाति किञ्चन न तद श्नाति कश्चन ॥ ८ ॥

"9. It is by the blessed government of that indestructible and eternal Being, that the sun and the moon follow their regular courses, that the solar system is balanced in its position, that the periodicity of time—*nimesha*, *muhurta*, day and night, fortnight, month, season, etc.,—follows in succession, that the easterly rivers flow from the snow-covered mountains towards the east, and the westerly rivers flow towards the west, that men admire generous men, that the gods respond to prayers, and that departed ancestors incline towards the purified offerings made to them."

एतस्य वा अक्षरस्य प्रशासने गार्गि सूर्य्याचन्द्रमसौ विधृतौ तिष्ठत एतस्य वा अक्षरस्य प्रशासने गार्गि द्यावापृथिव्यौ विधृते तिष्ठत एतस्य वा अक्षरस्य प्रशासने गार्गि निमेषा मुहूर्त्ता अहोरात्राण्यर्द्धमासा मासा ऋतवः संवत्सरा इति विधृतास्तिष्ठन्त्येतस्य वा अक्षरस्य प्रशासने गार्गि प्राच्योऽन्या नद्यः स्यन्दन्ते श्वेतेभ्यः पर्वतेभ्यः प्रतीच्योऽन्या यां याञ्च दिशमन्वेति एतस्य वा अक्षरस्य प्रशासने गार्गि ददतो मनुष्याः प्रशंसन्ति यजमानं देवो दर्वीं पितरोऽन्वायत्ताः ॥ ९ ॥

Again in the fourth Chapter, 5th Brahmana :—†

"7. All that makes the Brahmanas, the Kshatriyas, these Lokas, these Devas, these Vedas and this material world, all this is in the Great Soul."

'8. Just as when you beat a drum, you cannot catch the sound that proceeds from it, but you catch the sound, if you catch hold of the drum or the beater."

"9. Just as when you blow a conch-shell, you cannot catch the sound that proceeds from the conch, but you catch the sound, if you catch hold of the conch or the blower."

"10. Just as when you play upon a violin,

---

† * * * इदं ब्रह्मेदं क्षत्त्रमिमे लोका इमे देवा इमे वेदा इमानि भूतानीदं सर्व्वं यदयमात्मा ॥ ७ ॥

स यथा दुन्दुभेर्हन्यमानस्य न बाह्याञ्छब्दाञ्छक्नुयाद्ग्रहणाय दुन्दुभेस्तु ग्रहणेन दुन्दुभ्याघातस्य वा शब्दो गृहीतः ॥ ८ ॥

स यथा शङ्खस्य ध्मायमानस्य न बाह्याञ्छब्दाञ्छक्नुयाद्ग्रहणाय शङ्खस्य तु ग्रहणेन शङ्खध्मस्य वा शब्दो गृहीतः ॥ ९ ॥

स यथा वीणायै वाद्यमानायै न बाह्याञ्छब्दाञ्छक्नुयाद

you cannot catch the sound that proceeds from it, but you catch the sound if you catch hold of the violin or the player."

"11. Just as the smoke, rising from the burning of wet wood, spreads in the sky in various shapes, so Maitreyi, in this Universe, the Identical One breathes life into different forms. In fact, all this is inspired by Him, the Great Inspirer of life, &c."

The manner in which the presence of the one and same God is felt in all things can, no doubt, be understood by the figures of speech given above. As sound, which is invisible, can be felt in diverse things, when you adopt a particular means, so the existence of the Supreme Being though invisible, may be felt in all things, if you adopt a particular means.

But what is the particular means? It is

ग्रहणाय वीणायै तु ग्रहणेन वीणावादस्य वा शब्दो गृहीतः ॥ १० ॥

स यथार्द्रैधाग्नेरभ्याहितस्य पृथग्धूमा विनिश्चरन्त्येवं वा अरेऽस्य महतो भूतस्य निश्वसितं * * * सर्वाणि च भूतान्यस्यै वैतानि सर्वाणि निश्वसितानि ॥

devotion and prayer. See how in the following hymn of the Rigveda (Sukta 12, Mandal 11), the devotee vivified with Bhakti (reverential emotion) beholds the God in a personal shape, named as Indra, not only as inspiring all nature with life and as giving order to it, but also as being directly in touch with the human heart, as regards all its requirements.

"1. Ye men! He, who taking the form of one born, becomes the leader of men and of gods, who adorned the gods with valour, before whom the universe trembled—that mighty leader of hosts is Indra.'

"2. Ye men! He, who made the trepidating earth firm, who made the raging mountains steady, who made the huge firmament, who fixed the heavens in their places, is verily the Indra.

"3. Ye men! He, who by confounding the snake-like clouds caused the seven rivers to flow, who set free the lights, who were like cows confined by force, who causes the lightining to flash between two places of cloud, and to whom is due the destruction of hostile armies, is verily the Indra."

"4. Ye men! He, who made this perishable universe, who has placed the savage nations in some remote corner, who even as a hunter achieves a thousand conquests over those who ought to be conquered, and thus takes away their resources, is verily the Indra."

"5. Ye men! That mysterious Being, of whom people say,—where is He? of whom people even say that he does not exist, who like a true chastiser deprives the wicked of their resources, is verily the Indra."

"6. Ye men! He, who bestows prosperity, who gives wealth unto the poor, the beggar and the religious bard, who protects the worshipper earnestly engaged in the meritorious acts of worship, is verily the Indra."

"7. Ye men! He, who guides the instincts of horses, cattle, communities, and all that carry them, who made the sun to shine and the dawn to break, and who pours down water, is verily the Indra."

"8. Ye men! He, whom rival armies both invoke, and the good and the bad both in antagonism invoke, whom two persons in the same car both invoke differently, is verily the Indra."

"9. Ye men! He, without whom no man can achieve success, whose aid people invoke for protection on the battle-field, in whom is the trust of the whole world, and who destroys even the undecaying mountains, is verily the Indra."

"10. Ye men! He, who confounded legions of wicked and sinful unbelievers, who refuses success to the arrogant, and who destroys the enemies of honest men, is verily the Indra."

"11. Ye men! He, who discovered *Shambara* hidden in a mountain after forty years and who destroyed the strong monster named *Ahi* or the snake, is verily the Indra."

"12, Ye men! He, who has in Him the seven rays (colours), who sends down showers to fulfil desires, who is strong, who causes the even rivers to flow, who destroys with thunder Rouhina that wanted to enter heaven by force, is verily the Indra."

There are some more verses in this hymn but as they have some technical allusion, they are not reproduced here.

SECTION 6.—THE TWO-FOLD REVELATIONS OF THE VEDAS CONTINUED.

ONE more instance of the Rational Revelation of the Vedas and one more instancc of Emotional Revelation contained in them, are given below.

In Swetaswatara Upanished of the Krishna Yajurvada (Chapter 1), is the following :—*

"8. The God of the universe maintains this universe, produced by the contact of the destructible and the indestuctible, of the manifest and the unmanifest. The human soul, though primarily not the author of any activity, falls into a state of bondage, because it enjoys and suffers. But man is extricated from that bondage, as soon as he truly knows the Supreme Deity."

"9. The Omniscient Soul and the ignorant soul are both beginningless, though

---

* संयुक्तमेतत् क्षरमक्षरञ्च व्यक्ताव्यक्तं भरते विश्वमीशः। अनीशश्चात्मा वध्यते भोक्तृभावाज्ज्ञात्वा देवं मुच्यते सर्वपाशैः ॥ ८ ॥

ज्ञाज्ञौ द्वावजावीशानीशावजा ह्येका भोक्तृभोग्यार्थ-

the one is the Lord, and the other servant. The pristine and pure Nature is also beginningless, on which the human soul, though primarily no actor, hangs, when one knows the Supreme Lord, the human soul and nature—then only he reaches Brahma."

"10. Perishable nature and the imperishable and undecaying soul have one and the same God as their Lord. When one loves Him, fixes himself on Him and makes himself at one with Him, then comes about the cessation of the world of delusion."

"11. When one knows that Supreme Lord, all ties are broken, the pains arising from ignorance cease, and the change of birth and death cease, etc., etc."

युक्ता। अनन्तश्चात्मा विश्वरूपो ह्यकर्त्ता त्रयं यदा विन्दते ब्रह्ममेतत् ॥ ९ ॥

क्षरं प्रधानममृताक्षरं हरः क्षरात्मानावीशते देव एकः। तस्याभिध्यानाद् योजनात् तत्त्वभावाद् भूयश्चान्ते विश्वमायानिवृत्तिः ॥ १० ॥

ज्ञात्वा देवं सर्वपाशापहानिः क्षीणैः क्लेशैर्जन्ममृत्युप्रहाणिः। तस्याभिध्यानात्तृतीयं देहभेदे विश्वैश्वर्यं केवल आप्तकामः ॥ ११ ॥

In Rigveda, (10th Mandal, 121st Sukta,) is the following earnest longing to worship the Lord of the Creation, thus furnishing a sublime instance of emotionalism.

"1 Whom shall we worship but Him, who existed at the beginning as *Hiranyagarbha*, who taking a form and shape at once became the Lord of the creation, and who placed the earth and the firmament each in its place?"

"2. Whom shall we worship but Him, who gave the soul its strength, whose orders all *Devatas* obey, whose shadow is immortality, and whose slave is death?"

"3. Whom shall we worship but Him, who is the sole King of the seeing and living creation, and who is the Lord of the bipeds and quadrupeds?"

"4. Whom shall we worship but Him, by whose greatness the snow-covered hills were made, as whose creation the watery ocean is known, and the extension of whose arms is space in this or that direction?"

"5. Whom shall we worship but Him, who established this firm earth and this upheaved heaven, who keeps suspended the heavenly world and the world above that, and who measured the worlds yet above?"

"6. Whom shall we worship but Him, who caused the universe musically and beautifully to pose, and whom the bright universe feels as the giorious, and by whose power the sun rises and shines?"

"7. Whom shall we worship but Him, who brought Himself into existence as the life of all *Devatas*, when the immense sheet of water covering the universe conceived and produced heat and fire?"

"8. Whom shall we worship but Him, who looked upon the surface of the water, and it produced vitality and force by imbibing strength from Him, and by thus looking on became the Paramount Lord of all Devatas?"

"9. Whom shall we worship but Him, who is the creator of this world, whose power of support is ceaseless, who made the sky, and who made this plenty of refreshing water. May He be gracious to us."

"10. Thou Lord of all creatures! None but Thee has created all these things. May our object in making this sacrifice be fulfilled May we obtain the objects of our heart."

SECTION 7.—THE KARMA KANDA OF THE VEDAS.

IN the foregoing sections the hymns or prayers have alone been referred to, to illustrate the emotionol revelation or the Karma Kanda of the Vedas. But the hymns are not the only elements of Karma Kanda. They are attended with *Yagnas* or sacrifices and other ceremonies. Now no one can doubt that a sacrificing spirit is the best means of purifying the heart and ensuring and testing earnestness. The offers of even humble earthly objects as sacrifices develope a sacrificing tendenoy and is thus spiritually useful.

Then, as regards other ceremonies. Ceremonies are the handmaids of devotionalism. They are thus a main part of Karma Kanda. They develope and invigorate devotion. They serve to concentrate attention and to prevent distraction and dissipation. Thus they are of very great use and importance.

Ceremonies sometimes degenrate into dead forms and idle pretences. But degeneration is possible in everything. Everything is capable of being abused. It is an abuse of ceremony, when in the observance of it, there is no life in the shape of earnestness and devotion. In such cases ceremonies may be justly condemned and despised.

But real ceremonies are great helps to *Sadhana* or spiritual education. In temporal matters ceremonies are resorted to, to make an impression or to point off the beginning or the end of a thing. They impart the sweetness and pleasantness of poetry to things, which without them, would be dry and prosaic and irksome. When this is so in worldly matters, there can be no doubt as to the utility of ceremony in matters devotional. The spirit is invisble. Spiritual truths are often intangible. Ceremonies give them a local habitation and a name and fix a time for them. Thus the sacrifice that a devotee makes to his God, though it should really consist of his love, gratefulness and praise, is advantageously put in the shape of ceremonies. These ceremonies make tangible what is intangible. They give a material shape to spiritual offerings made by a worshipper out of the earnestness of his heart.

The ceremonies of worship are called *Yagnas.* Various *Yagnas* used to be performed in the olden times. They were all sacrifices of some kind or other.

But the sacrifice or *Yagna* of love was the *Yagna* which Sree Krishna taught mankind to make. He was called *Yagneshwara,* the Lord of *Yagna.* But Lord of what *Yagna* ? The *Yagna* of *Prem-bhakti* (the sacrifice of love)

Even the sacrifice of love is assisted by ceremonies. Sri Gauranga enjoined that in the place of all other *Yagnas* and ceremonies, the *Nama Yagna,* i. e., the chanting of *Hari nama* and the *Sankirtana* (singing devotional songs in chorus) should be substituted in the present age, in which the name of *Hari* only was the be-all and end-all for all purposes of salvation. § the *Vaidika Yagnas* fell into disuse

---

§ हरेर्नाम हरेर्नाम हरेर्नामैव केवलम् ।

—*Brihannaradiya Purana.*

because they were performed not directly to please the God of the human heart, but to secure *swarga,*—meaning heavenly happiness. '*Swarga Kama yayita*'—sacrifice for heavenly bliss.' But this view of the *Vaidika yagnas* is not quite correct. For the Mimansa philosophy explains that heavenly happiness is to be sought not as an object of selfish gratification, but because it is the highest duty enjoined.

CHAPTER V.

THE DOUBLE REVELATION AS REALIZED IN THE BRAHMANICAL PERIOD.

Section 1.—The Brahmanic Period Generally.

The grandest revolution that occurred in India, and in fact, in the whole world, is the Brahmanical revolution which followed the Vedic age. It was a revolution by which the highest truths of both Rationalism and Emotionalism were typified and named. As regards Rationalism, the highest and the sublimest generalization of it was condensed in that sacred formula, the *Gayatri*, which was framed to concentrate thought and attention upon the one Spiritual Essence of heaven and the earth, and of the world between.

As regards emotionalism, the successors of the Rishis vividly realized God as personally regent on this earth and pouring blessings upon man. Revealed as such they called Him *Sri Vishnu*. Some called Him as well as by the name of *Shiva*.

Thus they realized the Supreme Being, not only rationally as the spiritual sun of the three *lokas* (worlds), but also emotionally as the all-skilful and all-powerful, and as the all-loving and all-beautiful Personal God of the creation—*Vishnu*—the Central Personality of the universe, who should be worshipped and loved.

Signs and symbols are necessary and useful in material sciences, to fix and to localize abstract truths and conclusions. They are equally necessary and useful in spiritual science. Thus the syllable, '*Om*', adopted by the Brahmanas as symbolizing the Supreme Being, rendered the greatest service to them, in respect of spiritual development and progress. And as the syllable, 'Om', was the verbal symbol, the *Nârayana chakra* (*the Shâlagrâma*) was the visible symbol of the Supreme Being. In certain quarters, the phallic symbol was also adopted as typifying the creative energy of God. These symbols tend to assist *Bhakti* or emotionalism, though primarily inspired by rationalism and abstract conceptions. What emotionalism wants, is to realize the Divine

Being in a personal form, responding to its requirements. All religions are more or less based on such a realization; and the real religion of the Brahmanas consisted of the realization of the Supreme Being in the Personal form of Sri Vishnu. The Supreme Being is revealed both as personal and impersonal.* To say, that He is only impersonal and not personal, is to impute imperfection to Him, just as to say the reverse.

In the Manu-Sanhita (Chapter 1, Verse 17) is the following:—

"17. The Supreme Being appears to the wise with a body, as the materials which form body, *viz.*, the five *tanmatras*, &c., as combined with the elements, &c., come from Him."†

Again Sri Vishnu, as holding in his hands *sankha*, *chakra*, *gada* and *padma*, *i.e.*, the symbols of harmony, intelligential power,

---

* सगुणो निर्गुणो विष्णुर्ज्ञानगम्योह्यसौ स्मृतः ।

—*Vedanta-tattwasara.*

† यन्मूर्त्यवयवाः सूक्ष्मास्तस्येमान्याश्रयन्ति षट् ।
तस्माच्छरीरमित्याहुस्तस्य मूर्त्तिं मनीषिणः ॥ १७ ॥

physical force and love, is revealed to emotionalism or *Bhakti*.

In the Adhyatma Ramayana is the following:—

"It is only when, one feels sincere *Bhakti* (reverence and love) to Vishnu, that his intellect is purified by His grace, and he acquires pure truth, and is then blessed with beatitude."*

The Bhagavat Purana has it :—

"When the Gracious Lord Vishnu is pleased, it is then only, man becomes free from the influences of gross nature, and seeks union with Him."†

Section 2.—The Gnana and the Bhakti Kanda of the Brahmanical Period.

In every Sanhita and in every Purana, there are distinct texts of rationalistic

---

* विष्णोर्हि भक्तिः सुविशोधनं धिय-
स्ततो भवेज्ज्ञानमतीव निर्म्मलम् ।
विशुद्धतत्त्वानुभवोभवेत्ततः
सम्यग्विदित्वा परमं पदं व्रजेत् ॥ ३२ ॥

† सम्प्रसन्ने भगवति पुरुषः प्राकृतैर्गुणैः ।

Hinduism. The Brahma Baibarta Purana thus speaks of the importance of rationalism:—

"11. The essence of all philosophy, *i. e.*, divine knowledge, is that which opens the spiritual eyes of the ignorant, and destroys doubts and confusion."*

It is, however, the *Bhakti Kanda* of the *Bhakti Yoga*, which practically elevated the Brahmanas into that high sphere of energy and activity which they displayed. Says the Vishnu Purana (III-4-6):—

"6 If one worships Sri Vishnu, all his desires are fulfilled and he becomes fitted for heaven, and attains the best salvation."†

Thus the heart of the Brahmanas, was filled with love and reverence to Sri Vishnu as the source of all strength, the source of all beauty and happiness. His bosom swell-

---

विमुक्तो जीवनिर्मुक्तो ब्रह्मनिर्वाणमृच्छति ॥१४॥

*सारभूतश्च तत्त्वानामज्ञानान्धकलोचनम् ।
द्वैधभ्रम तमोध्वंस सुप्रकृष्ट प्रदीपकम् ॥ ११ ॥

†भौमान् मनोरथान् स्वर्गान्, स्वर्गिवन्धं तथास्पदम् ।
प्राप्नोत्याराधिते विष्णौ निर्वाणमपि चोत्तमम् ॥ ६ ॥

ed with this love and reverence and made strong both morally and physically. Such a faith is calculated to make individual as well as nations great. Strengthened by this faith the first Brahmanical leader *Parashuram* established the kingdom of spirituality over the whole of that portion of India which was inhabited by the Aryans, defeating several times those mighty Aryan races called the Kshatriyas, who prided themselves on brute force, and disdained the spiritual civilization of the Brahmanas.

Sri Vishnu was worshipped by the spiritually advanced Brahmanas with *Nishkam Prem* (disinterested love). Others worshipped Him for worldly benefits. Both classes got satisfaction.

"All must equally worship the supreme person Sri Vishnu, those who desire nothing, those who desire everything, or those far-sighted persons who desire salvation." *

---

* अकामः सर्वकामो वा मोक्षकाम उदारधीः ।
तीव्रेण भक्तियोगेन यजेत पुरुषं परम् ॥ १० ॥

Bhagavat Purana, (2-3-10).

"By prayer to the Almighty Vishnu, whatever a man desires, great or small, is obtained by him." †

Section 3.—Avatarism, Rational and Emotional.

It has been seen that in the Vedas, *Bhakti Kanda* or emotionslism realizes the Supreme Being as in the elements or the Devatas. The Bhakti Kanda of the Brahmanical period realizes the Supreme Being as Incarnations.

The Incarnations of Sri Vishnu may be classed under two heads: (1) Incarnations in the process of creation, and (2) Incarnations by a certain law of Grace for the benefit of men. The first class may be called Revelations of Rationalism, the second class Revelations of Emotionalism.

When the first individual of each class of

---

† यद्यदिच्छति यावच्च फलमाराधितेऽच्युते ।
तत् तदाप्नोति राजेन्द्र भूरि स्वल्पमथापि वा ॥७॥

Vishnu Purana, (3-8-7).

beings was brought into existence, he was a miracle, he came out fresh as an emanation from the Divine Will. The cover of Maya did not sit thick upon him. He was, in short, an Incarnation of the Deity. Thus the first man, Manu, was an Incarnation, the first fish was an Incarnation, the first amphibious creature, the first quadruped, and so on. It is thus that all the creatures of the world are, according to Hinduism, the descendants of the first Incarnation of each kind. Men are the descendants of His first Human Incarnation, the beasts and birds and all other creatures are descendants of His other Incarnations. Thus all are kith and kin. All should be felt or regarded as forming one common family,—men, beasts, birds and all,—all coming from one common stock, Sri Vishnu, Who cherishes all, loves all and sports with all.

The second class of Incarnations, *viz.*, those that are associated with emotionalism or *Bhakti*, are those cases, in which by the Divine Law of Grace enunciated by the *Bhagavat Geeta* (Ch. IV), God-men are born from time to time to manifest the Presence and the Reality of the Almighty, among men, in order to prevent them from falling. *

"7. Whenever there is decay of *dharma*, Oh Bharata, and there is exaltation of *adharma*, then I myself come forth."

"8. For the protection of the good, for the destruction of evil-doers, for the sake of firmly establishing *dharma*, I am born from age to age."

In the records of the world, it is seen that men are born now and then on this earth, who like comets shed an overpowering spiritual lustre over the whole of humanity for a time, and then leaves it to utilize that lustre for ages. Such a phenomenon has taken place in all ages and in all countries. The Rationalists would call these phenomena 'great men,' while the Emotionalists would call them *Avatars* or Incarnations. Call them 'great men' or *Avatars*, the fact remains that

---

* यदा यदा हि धर्मस्य ग्लानिर्भवति भारत ।
अभ्युत्थानमधर्मस्य तदाऽत्मानं सृज्याम्यहम् ॥७॥
परित्राणाय साधूनां विनाशाय च दुष्कृताम् ।
धर्मसंस्थापनार्थाय सम्भवामि युगे युगे ॥ ८ ॥

the men among whom they are born and their successors, see vividly God through them and in them. If their power, goodness and purity be so unique, so infinite-like, so transcendental, as to make them decidedly above humanity, how can the *Bhaktas* (men of devotion) help bowing to them as *Avatars* or Incarnations.

Besides, one thing is observed in these Avatars. They do not attain to their transcendental position by effort and struggle. They are born with it. They are not their masters, but are forced to their godly position by things beyond their own control. They not only teach about God, but their acts impress themselves upon those around, as direct acts of God, and their words as His direct words. Besides, they are also impelled to testify themselves as being God-men. Such Incarnations cannot be chance-work, but must constitute the fulfilment of a law as enunciated by the Bhagavat Geeta. As God is all-good and all-powerful, and mysterious are his ways, there is nothing perplexing in the belief that the God-head, in some cases, assumes the form of man without his short-comings.

Even if these God-men be not *Avatars* or Incarnations of God, in any particular sense, yet they see God face to face and touch Him tangibly. They are, therefore, saviours, to reach whom is to reach God, and to praise whom is to praise God, especially as there can be no doubt about the following great spiritual truth.

"As men approach and serve Me, so do I approach and serve men." *

Section 4.—The Double Revelation as Realized in the Brahmanical Period.

THE Rationalism of the Brahmanical or post-Vedic period, is thus expressed in the Manu Sanhita, Chapter XII, Verses 122 to 125: ‡—

"122. That Invisible Supreme Person is the object of contemplation, Who is regula-

---

* ये यथा मां प्रपद्यन्ते तांस्तथैव भजाम्यहम्।

Geeta, (4-11).

‡ प्रशासितारं सर्वेषामणीयांसमणोरपि।
रुक्माभं स्वप्नधीगम्यं विद्यात्तं पुरुषं परम्॥२२॥

tor of all, is finer than the finest atom, is full of golden rays being all consciousness and is seen by the mind's eye in a state of ecstacy."

"123. This Supreme Soul is called by some *Agni*, by some *Manu*, the Lord of creation, by some worshipped as *Indra*, by some as the *Life*, and by some as the *Eternal Brahma*."

"124. This Supreme Soul pervades all things in fine forms, making them rotate like wheels, through formation, growth and destruction."

"125. He who sees by his mind's eye the Supreme Soul thus pervading all universe, becomes perfectly harmonized and attains the state of beatitude."

The above is religious teaching or *Gnana Kanda*. The *Bhakti Kanda* or religion

---

एतमेके वदन्त्यग्निं मनुमन्ये प्रजापतिम् ।
इन्द्रमेके परे प्राणमपरे ब्रह्म शाश्वतम् ॥१२३॥
एष सर्वाणि भूतानि पञ्चभिर्व्याप्य मूर्त्तिभिः ।
जन्मवृद्धिक्षयैर्नित्यं संसारयति चक्रवत् ॥१२४॥
एवं यः सर्वभूतेषु पश्यत्यात्मानमात्मना ।
स सर्वसमतामेत्य ब्रह्माभ्येति परं पदम् ॥१२५॥

proper, of the Brahamans, that which swelled their bosom, and made them unconquerable, is found in their Vishnu Bhakti, as appears in the following lines of the Vishnu Smriti, Chapter 98 :—

"Om, adoration be to Thee, Thou art the God of the gods, the God of the world—Vasudeva, the God that wert in the begining, the God of Love, the Guardian of the earth. There is neither beginning, nor middle, nor end in Thee. Thou art the Lord, the Good Lord, the great Lord of creatures ; Thou art the Lord of strength and of speech, and the Lord of the terrestial world and of the heavens, the Lord of the woods, and of the showers of rain ; Thou art the Lord of the earth, of the waters, of the eight quarters of the skies, and of the principal *mahat* ; Thou art the Lord of the wind, and of prosperity ; Thou as Brahma art dear to Brahmanas ; Thou pervadest everything, surpassing all conception, and attainable by meditation ; Thou art invoked at numberless offerings, &c. &c." *

---

* ओँ नमस्ते देवदेव वासुदेव आदिदेव कामदेव

The statement that the *Bhakti Kanda* or religion proper of the Brahmanas, consists of their Vishnu *Bhakti*, requires a word of explanation. Vast as the country of the Brahmanas is, it is only natural that differences should arise in their modes of worship and in respect of the name of the Deity adopted in worshipping. Thus, sects were formed, one of which adopted the name Siva and others adopted other names virtually as synonyms of Sri Vishnu—the Supreme Personality of infinite love and endless power. In this state of things some religious teachers wanted to make their writings catholic, and attempted to reconcile the different names and the various associations of belief as different phases of the same thing. Others again, each of whom had belief in one name as that of the Supreme Being and in one form

---

महीपाल अनादिमध्यनिधन प्रजापते सुप्रजापते महाप्रजापते ऊर्ज्जस्पते वाचस्पते जगत्पते दिवस्पते वनस्पते पयस्पते पृथिवीपते सलिलपते दिक्पते महत्पते मरुत्पते लक्ष्मीपते ब्रह्मरूप ब्राह्मणप्रिय सर्वग अचिन्त्य ज्ञानगम्य पुरुहूत इत्यादि ।

of worship as the best, and regarded the other names and other forms as subordinate—effected a reconcilement in that way. Some *shastra*-makers of a more philosophical disposition again explained all the names as meaning each a limited Divine function and thus taught the doctrines, of Trinity and the like. These doctrines, however, do not touch either the real religion or the general philosophy of religion of the Hindus. They only serve to unite and cement religious tales and stories into a common structure.

Section 5.—The double Revelation of the Brahmanical Period continued :

It is seen that the Rationalism of this period is the same as in the Vedas, *i. e.* the Upanishads. The Revelations of the Upanishads, no Brahman could or did question. The truths of the Upanishads are simply reproduced in later Brahmanical books. The following passage from the Vishnu Purana (Book VI, Chapter V 66-68) embodies many of those spiritual truths and illustrates the Hindu science of spirituality :—*

"The wise contemplate Him, who is inexpressible, without beginning, transcending thoughts, imperishable, unchangeable, whose personality is undefined, who is without limbs, who is the lord of all, all-pervading, eternal, who is the cause of all material existences, the support of all, and who has none to support him and from whom all creatures have sprung into being. He is the Supreme Spirit, He is the Supreme Destination, He is the object of worship by those who seek salvation, He is the Finest *Essence* declared by the Vedas, He is Vishnu, He is the highest object of attainment."

The *Bhakti Kânda* or devotionalism of the Brahmanas of the same period, is em-

---

* यत्तदव्यक्तमजरमचिन्त्यमजमव्ययम् ।
अनिर्देश्यमरूपञ्च पाणिपादाद्यसंयुतम् ॥६६॥
विभूं सर्वगतं नित्यं भूतयोनिमकारणम् ।
व्याप्यव्याप्तं यतः सर्वंतद्वै पश्यन्ति सूरयः ॥६७॥
तद् ब्रह्म परमंधाम तत् ध्येयं मोक्षकाङ्क्षिणा ।
श्रुतिवाक्योदितं सूक्ष्मं तद्विष्णोः परमंपदम् ॥६८॥

bodied in numerous *Shâstras*. Having reproduced the hymn to Sri Vishnu in the Vishnu *Sanhitâ* in the preceding section, the following passage is reproduced from the Brihat Harita Sanhita (Chapter I) relating to the worship of Sri Vishnu :—*

"Listen, O king! Listen to the purport of the Vedas as communicated to me by *Brahma*. I will tell the now, what constitute the Supreme Religion, and so listen with rapt attention."

"Vishnu, called also Janârdana, is, of all the gods, the Supreme God without a beginning."

"He is the God, the eternal Lord of the universe, the Nârâyana, the Vasudeva and the Hari of the devotees."

"There are four blessed means by which the pure-minded can reach Him, and it is

---

* शृणु राजन्! प्रवक्ष्यामि सर्वं वेदोपबृंहितम्।
यदुक्तं ब्रह्मणा पूर्वं पृच्छतो मम भूपते॥
तद्ब्रवीमि परं धर्म्मं शृणुष्वैकाग्रमानसः।
सर्वेषामेव देवानामनादिः पुरुषोत्तमः॥

beyond doubt that the transcendental goal can be attained by *Bhakti* alone."

"The spiritually advanced, according to their higher capacities, form a standard of *Bhakti* which is very high, but for the generality of mankind, worshipping God with the obedience of a servant is more natural."

"The Almighty is the master and His creatures are servants and this relationship exists naturally."

"This worship as by a servant is the highest religion and is the highest good. The final release is caused by it. Hell is the portion of those who follow any other course."

ईश्वरस्तु स एवान्यं जगतो विभुरव्ययः ।
नारायणो वासुदेवो विष्णुर्ब्रह्मात्मनो हरिः ॥
चतुर्भिः शोभनोपायैः साध्योऽयं सुमहात्मनः ।
तुरीयपदयोर्भक्त्या सुसिद्धोऽयमुदाहृतः ॥
तं स्वीकुर्वन्ति विद्वांसः स्वस्वरूपतया सदा ।
नैसर्गिकं हि सर्वेषां दास्यमेव हरेः सदा ॥
स्वाम्यं परस्वरूपं स्याद्दास्यं जीवस्य सर्वदा ।
प्रकृत्या त्वात्मनो रूपं स्वाम्यं दास्यमिति स्थितिः ॥

"This submissive worship of God is the highest Bhakti and the touch of a person without Bhakti hurls a Brahmana, O king, down to the hell."

"The wretches, who do not worship God like a servant, are certainly turned into Chandals during their very life-time."

"Therefore, O holy king, worship God with willing submission ('dasya bhakti'] and do thine daily work and observe the ceremonials only for pleasing the Almighty."

दास्यमेव परं धर्म्मं दास्यमेव परं हितम् ।
दास्येनैव भवेन्मुक्तिरन्यथा निरयं भवेत् ॥
विष्णोर्दास्यं परा भक्तिरेषा तु न भवेत् क्वचित् ।
तेषामेव हि संस्पृष्टं निरयं ब्राह्मणा नृप ॥
नारायणस्य दासा ये न भवन्ति नराधमाः ।
जीवन्त एव चण्डाला भविष्यन्ति न संशयः ॥
तस्माद्दास्यं परां भक्तिमालम्ब्य नृपसत्तम ।
नित्यं नैमित्तिकं सर्वं कुर्य्यात् प्रीत्यै हरेः सदा ॥

CHAPTER V.

THE TWO REVELATIONS AS IN THE SRIMAT BHAGAVAT GEETA.

Section 1.—The Gnana Kanda of the Geeta.

THE *Gnana Kânda* or the Revelation of Rationalism is expressed in the Geeta in terms similar to those of the Upanishads. In Chapter VII, Verses 7 to 13 are the following :—*

"7. There is nought whatsoever higher than I *i.e.* God. All this is woven in God, as multitudes of jewels on a string."

"8. God is the wateriness of water, radiance of the moon and the sun, *Pranava* of the Vedas, sound of the air, and manliness of man."

"9. God is the sweet odour of the odoriferous, brilliance of the bright, life of all living things and ascetism of ascetics.

"10 God is the Eternal seed of all things,

---

* मत्तः परतरं नान्यत् किञ्चिदस्ति धनञ्जय ।
मयि सर्वमिदं प्रोतं सूत्रे मणिगणा इव ॥७॥

the intelligence of the intelligent and the splendour of the splendid."

"11. God is the strength of the strong without passionateness or irritability, and also supplies desires in men who are pure-hearted."

"12. The three tendencies of *Sattwa Rajas* and *Tamas* are in God and God is not in them."

"13. All this world, deluded by these three tendencies, does not know God, who is above these tendencies and is imperishable."

The following passages, in Chapters VII and IX, among others of the same kind, also more or less relate to the *Gnana Kânda.*

रसोऽहमप्सु कौन्तेय प्रभाऽस्मि शशिसूर्य्ययोः ।
प्रणवः सर्व्वबेदेषु शब्दः खे पौरुषं नृषु ॥८॥
पुण्योगन्धः पृथिव्याञ्च तेजश्चास्मि विभावसौ ।
जीवनं सर्व्वभूतेषु तपश्चास्मि तपस्विषु ॥९॥
बीजं मां सर्व्वभूतानां विद्धि पार्थ सनातनम् ।
बुद्धिर्बुद्धिमतामस्मि तेजस्तेजस्विनामहम् ॥१०॥
बलं बलवतामस्मि कामरागविवर्जितम् ।
धर्म्माविरुद्धो भूतेषु कामोऽस्मि भरतर्षभ ॥११॥

These passages, however, show in the clearest manner how Nature's God stands in relation to Nature in the state of purity, called *Yoga-maya*. In showing this, these passages form the stepping-stone to the Revelation of Emotionalism or *Bhakti*.

"14. This Divine *Maya* of God, consisting of the three *Gunas*, is hard to pierce. They who come to Sri Krishna as He is manifest in person, they only cross over this *Maya*." *

"25. God is not discovered to all, He being enveloped in His *Yoga-māya*. This deluded world knoweth Him not, the Unborn and the Imperishable, in Sri Krishna, *i.* God manifest in person."

"4. By the unmanifest Supreme Being

ये चैव सात्त्विका भावा राजसास्तामसाश्च ये ।
मत्त एवेति तान्विद्धि न त्वहं तेषु ते मयि ॥१२॥
त्रिभिर्गुणमयैर्भावैरेभिः सर्वमिदं जगत् ।
मोहितं नाभिजानाति मामेभ्यः परमव्ययम् ॥१३॥

* दैवी ह्येषा गुणमयी मम माया दुरत्यया ।
मामेव ये प्रपद्यन्ते मायामेतां तरन्ति ते ॥१४॥

all this world is spread out, all beings live in God, but God is not in them."

"5. That all beings are in God, you must not see, but see only this Divine mystery that God supports all beings and is their efficient cause and yet He is not in them."

"6. Just as the ether ever in the sky moves everywhere, so know thou that all things have their being in Sri Krishna, or God manifest in person."

Thus the dogma about the *Adwaitabád* and the *Dwaitabád* is dismissed by Srimat Bhagavat Geeta.

नाहं प्रकाशः सर्वस्य योगमायासमावृतः ।
मूढ़ोऽयं नाभिजानाति लोको मामजमव्ययम् ॥२५॥

Geeta, Chapter 7.

मया ततमिदं सर्वं जगदव्यक्तमूर्त्तिना ।
मत्स्थानि सर्वभूतानि न चाहं तेष्ववस्थितः ॥४॥
न च मत्स्थानि भूतानि पश्य मे योगमैश्वरम् ।
भूतभृन्न च भूतस्थो ममात्मा भूतभावनः ॥५॥
यथाकाशस्थितो नित्यं वायुः सर्वत्रगो महान् ।
तथा सर्वाणि भूतानि मत्स्थानीत्युपधारय ॥६॥

Geeta, Chapter 9.

Section 2.—The Bhakti Kanda of the Geeta.

Having given a summary of the *Gnana Kânda* in the last section, the *Bhakti Kânda*, as treated in it may be now taken up. The Geeta is essentially a Revelation of *Bhakti* or of Emotionalism. It shows how God, as sought by the human heart, is found. The words of Divine friendship, addressed to Arjuna, are heard by every earnest devotee in the recesses of his heart as uttered by his own Supreme friend and Protector. In the *Gnana Kânda* man's relations with the Supreme being are more or less impersonal. In the *Bhakti Kânda* man seeks to realize his personal relations with Him, and when he does this, he finds Him as his Protector and his Friend, albeit the Supreme Ruler of the universe.

Man adores Him and loves Him and He helps and loves man.

The following verses explain the Bhakti Yoga and the manner in which the Emotional Revelation takes place:—

"29. He who has known me as the Lord of sacrifice and of penance, the mighty Ruler of all the worlds and the Lover of all beings, goeth to peace."*

"26. He who offereth to me, with devotion, a leaf, a flower, a fruit, water, I accept that as offered with devotion."†

"29. Who worships Me with Bhakti, in him I am, and he is in Me."‡

"34. Seek Me, worship Me and bow down to Me; and thus making yourself at one with Me, you, being devoted to Me, shall have Me."||

"47. Of those who have acquired a harmonized mind, he who worships Me with

---

* भोक्तारं यज्ञतपसां सर्वलोकमहेश्वरम् ।
सुहृदं सर्वभूतानां ज्ञात्वा मां शान्तिमृच्छति ॥२९॥

Geeta, Chapter 5.

† पत्रं पुष्पं फलं तोयं यो मे भक्त्या प्रयच्छति ।
तदहं भक्त्युपहृतमश्नामि प्रयतात्मनः ॥२६॥

‡ समोऽहं सर्व्वभूतेषु न मे द्वेष्योऽस्ति न प्रियः ।
ये भजन्ति तु मां भक्त्या मयि ते तेषु चाप्यहम् ॥२९॥

|| मन्मना भव मद्भक्तो मद्याजी मां नमस्कुरु ।
मामेवैष्यसि युक्त्वैवमात्मानं मत्परायणः ॥३४॥

Geeta, Chapter 9.

love, with all heart and soul, is the best harmonized in mind."*

If then to worship God with love, with all heart and soul is the best, the highest lot of man, in order to worship Him thus, it is necessary to find Him as the object of senses and as the object of his emotions. How and where to find Him as such?

Arjuna found Him in Sri Krishna Himself. He found the Almighty addressing him in person.

But all men requires to see him in some definite shape and form, in order to worship Him with love.

How are they to find Him so? The answer is found in the Sri Bhagavat Geeta. It says :— †

"20 & 21. Even as regards those who

---

* योगिनामपि सर्वेषां मद्गतेनान्तरात्मना ।
श्रद्धावान् भजते यो मां स मे युक्ततमो मत: ॥४७॥

Geeta, Chapter 6.

† कामैस्तैस्तैर्हृतज्ञाना: प्रपद्यन्तेऽन्यदेवता: ।
तं तं नियममास्थाय प्रकृत्या नियता: स्वया ॥२०॥

led by their nature under the influence of selfish objects, worship particular forms and shapes as *Devatâs*, I cause in them unfailing devotion to grow towards those shapes and forms, when they want to worship them with reverence and earnestness."

The Geeta then goes on to say,* "that the person who thus worships limited *Devatâs*, attain the object of their desire by My Grace, if they do it with sincere reverence." "But" it continues "the objects which such foolish men thus obtain, are of limited value; for, when worship is directed to limited powers (*Devatâs*), the worshippers

---

यो यो यां यां तनुं भक्तः श्रद्धयार्च्चितुमिच्छति ।
तस्य तस्याचलां श्रद्धां तामेव विदधाम्यहम् ॥२१॥

Geeta, Chapter 7.

* स तया श्रद्धया युक्तस्तस्याराधनमीहते ।
लभते च ततः कामान्मयैव विहितान् हि तान् ॥२२॥
अन्तवत्तु फलं तेषां तद्भवत्यल्पमेधसाम् ।
देवान्देवयजो यान्ति मद्भक्ता यान्ति मामपि ॥२३॥
अव्यक्तं व्यक्तिमापन्नं मन्यन्ते मामबुद्धयः ।
परं भावमजानन्तो ममाव्ययमनूत्तमम् ॥२४॥

Geeta, Chapter 7.

attain those limited powers only, while those who worship Me, attain Me. It is only the foolish who limit the limitless, not knowing My transcendental, lasting and supreme state."

Thus it appears, that when the object of worship is personalized, severing it from the conception of infinity and associating it with self-gratifying purposes, even then the Merciful Almighty promotes the earnestness and sincerity of the worshipper. It follows then, that when the worshipper personalizes the God of infinite power and goodness, as such, and worships Him disinterestedly in that personalized form and shape, He blesses and sanctions the worship by His real presence. In fact, the whole of the Geeta exemplifies how the sweet and loving God assures and comforts man, in a personal and living shape and form. Thus the disinterested worshipper of Supreme Lord finds Him so as to respond to his affections and senses.

Then in the next place, another question arises in connection with the Divine precept stated above, *viz.*, that to worship God with

Bhakti is the best thing that man can do. The question is this—the modes of thought and feeling are various in various men ; what is the right mode of worship then ? Sri Bhagavat Geeta (Chapter IV) answer this question as follows:—*

"10 & 11. Free thyself from fear, passion and infatuations and place thyself in My way and My protection, and be devoted to Me, purifying thyself by truth and discipline and then no matter in whatever way thou worshippest Me ; as thou worshippest so I respond, for what men really want lies in My way."

These sacred principles as enunciated in the Bhagavat Geeta, form the fundamental law of the *Bhakti Kânda* and the *Karma Kânda*.

God responds to the prayer of the worshipper, who prays to Him with a purified

---

* वीतरागभयक्रोधा मन्मया मामुपाश्रिताः ।
बह्वो ज्ञानतपसा पूता मद्भावमागताः ॥१०॥
ये यथा मां प्रपद्यन्ते तांस्तथैव भजाम्यहम् ।
मम वर्त्तानवर्त्तन्ते मनष्याः पार्थ सर्वशः ॥११॥

heart, perfectly surrendering himself to Him, and absorbed in contemplation of Him, whatever may be the form and the manner of the prayer and whatever the means adopted in making it.

For it is assured that, the diversity of ways and means that men follow to reach Him, are all His ways and means. But the conditions stated should not be overlooked. Those conditions exclude the wicked and the insincere from availing of this Law of Grace.

This Law thus plainly enunciated involves,—

1. The Great Principle of Toleration; and

2. The Great Principle that differences in forms of worship are immaterial provided there is earnestness and purity.

There is often bitter quarrel among men, whether the prophet followed by one is the true prophet or the prophet followed by another. The above Law sweeps off all occasions of any such controversy. For, even supposing that the prophet of one of the disputants is not a true prophet, if he worships God, with purity and earnestness of hearts, through that prophet he reaps all the advantages of having a true prophet.

Section 3.—Bhagavat Geeta, God in relation to the Universe and in relation to The Heart of Man.

God in relation to the universe awfully transcends the powers of the human mind. But God in relation to the human heart is the sweet and assuring Lord of his existence. In one case the relations of man with him are impersonal, in the other they are of a personal kind. In the one case it is only the intellect or the rational faculties that stir themselves after him, but their efforts are baffled and recoil. In the other, the heart and the emotional faculties follow Him, and bring back consolation and comfort. Sri Bhagavat Geeta (Chapter XI) illustrates this in the following passages.

God as appearing in the Infinite shape in relation to the universe. Says Arjuna:—*

"15. Within Thy Form, O God, the gods I see,
All gardes of beings with distinctive marks;
Brahma, the Lord, upon His lotus-throne,
The Rishis all and Serpents, the divine."

"16. With mouths, eyes, arms, breasts multitudinous,
I see Thee everywhere, unbounded Form
Beginning, middle, end, nor source of Thee,
Infinite Lord, Infinite Form, I find."

---

* अर्जुन उवाच ।—

पश्यामि देवांस्तव देव देहे
सर्वांस्तथा भूतविशेषसङ्घान् ।
ब्रह्माणमीशं कमलासनस्थ-
मृषींश्च सर्वानुरगांश्च दिव्यान् ॥ १५ ॥
अनेकबाहूदरवक्त्रनेत्रं
पश्यामि त्वां सर्वतोऽनन्तरूपम् ।
नान्तं न मध्यं न पुनस्तवादिं
पश्यामि विश्वेश्वर विश्वरूप ॥ १६ ॥

"17. Shining, a mass of splendour everywhere,
With discus, mace, tiara, I behold:
Blazing as fire, as sun, dazzling the gaze
From all sides in the sky, immeasurable."

"30. On every side, all-swallowing, fiery-tongued,
Thou lickest up mankind, devouring all;
Thy glory filleth space: The universe
Is burning, Vishnu, with Thy blazing rays."

किरीटिनं गदिनं चक्रिणञ्च
तेजोराशिं सर्वतो दीप्तिमन्तम् ।
पश्यामि त्वां दुर्निरीक्ष्यं समन्ताद्-
दीप्तानलार्कद्युतिमप्रमेयम् ॥ १७ ॥
लेलिह्यसे ग्रसमानः समन्ता-
ल्लोकान्समग्रान्वदनैर्ज्वलद्भिः ।
तेजोभिरापूर्य जगत्समग्रं
भासस्तवोग्राः प्रतपन्ति विष्णो ॥ ३० ॥
आख्याहि मे को भवानुग्ररूपो
नमोऽस्तु ते देववर प्रसीद ।
विज्ञातुमिच्छामि भवन्तमाद्यं
न हि प्रजानामि तव प्रवृत्तिम् ॥ ३१ ॥

At the above sight Arjuna being filled with wonder and fear thus prays to Sri Krishna to present himself in his former shape.

"31. Reveal Thy Self (as Sri Krishna) what awful form art Thou (now)?
I worship Thee! Have mercy, God supreme!
Thine inner Being I am fain to know;
This Thy forthstreaming Life bewilders me."

"45. I have seen That which none hath seen before,
My heart is glad, yet faileth me for fear;
Show me, O God, Thine other Form again,

अदृष्टपूर्वं हृषितोऽस्मि दृष्ट्वा
भयेन च प्रव्यथितं मनो मे ।
तदेव मे दर्शय देवरूपं
प्रसीद देवेश जगन्निवास ॥ ४५ ॥
किरीटिनं गदिनं चक्रहस्त-
मिच्छामि त्वां द्रष्टुमहं तथैव ।
तेनैव रूपेण चतुर्भुजेन
सहस्रवाहो भव विश्वमूर्ते ॥ ४६ ॥

Mercy, O God of gods, Home of all worlds."

"46. Diademed, mace and discus in Thy hand,
Again I fain would see Thee as before ;
Put on again Thy four-armed Shape, O Lord,
O Thousand-armed, of Forms innumerate."

Bhagavan says to Arjuna :—*

"47. Arjuna, by My favour thou hast seen,
This loftiest Form, by Yoga's self proclaimed!

---

* श्रीभगवानुवाच ।—

मया प्रसन्नेन तवार्जुनेदं
रूपं परं दर्शितमात्मयोगात् ।
तेजोमयं विश्वमनन्तमाद्यं
यन्मे त्वदन्येन न दृष्टपूर्वम् ॥ ४७ ॥
न वेदयज्ञाध्ययनैर्न दानै-
र्न च क्रियाभिर्न तपोभिरुग्रैः ।
एवं रूपः शक्य अहं नृलोके
द्रष्टुं त्वदन्येन कुरुप्रवीर ॥ ४८ ।

Radiant, all-penetrating, endless, first,
That none except thyself hath ever seen."

"48. Nor sacrifice nor Vedas, alms nor works,
Nor sharp austerity, nor study deep,
Can win the vision of this Form for man.
Foremost of Kurus, thou alone hast seen."

"49. Bacause thou hast behold this awful Form;
Cast fear away, and let thy heart rejoice;
Behold again mine own familiar Shape."

Thus saying Bhagavan assumed His former pleasing appearance and assured Arjuna's trembling heart. Whereupon Arjuna says :—*

"51 I am restored to peace and happi-

मा ते व्यथा मा च विमूढभावो
दृष्ट्वा रूपं घोरमीदृङ्ममेदम् ।
व्यपेतभीः प्रीतमनाः पुनस्त्वं
तदेव मे रूपमिदं प्रपश्य ॥ ४९ ॥

* अर्जुन उवाच ।—

दृष्ट्वेदं मानुषं रूपं तव सौम्यं जनार्दन ।
इदानीमस्मि संवृत्तः सचेताः प्रकृतिं गतः ॥ ५१ ॥

ness, seeing again that riendly human appearance of Yours."

Section 4.—Bhagavat Geeta reconciling the Nibritti-dharma of Gnana Yoga with the Prabritti-dharma of Karma Yoga.

It has been stated before that the Gnana Kanda is associated with Nibritti Dharma, *i. e.* the self-purification arising from contemplation and abstraction, and that the Karma Kanda (especially in the larger sense of the word Karma) is associated with the Prabritti Dharma, *i. e.* the self-purification arising from the performance of work done disinterestedly by way of sacrifice. In both, however, there is an abnegation of self. Nibritti is Gnana Yoga and Prabritti is Karma Yoga. Sri Bhagavat Geeta explains both. The following passages explain the Gnana Yoga :—*

---

* प्रजहाति यदा कामान्सर्वान् पार्थ मनोगतान् ।
आत्मन्येवात्मना तुष्टः स्थितप्रज्ञस्तदोच्यते ॥५५॥
दुःखेष्वनुद्विग्नमनाः सुखेषु विगतस्पृहः ।
वीतरागभयक्रोधः स्थितधीर्मुनिरुच्यते ॥ ५६ ॥

"55. When a man abandoneth, O Partha! all the desires of the heart and is satisfied in the Self by the Self, then is he called stable in mind."

"56. He whose mind is free from anxiety amid pains, indifferent amid pleasures, loosed from passion, fear and anger, he is called a Muni of stable mind."

"57. He who on every side is without attachments, whatever hap of fair and foul, who neither likes nor dislikes, of such a one the understanding is well-poised."

"58. When, again, as a tortoise draws in on all sides its limbs, he withdraws his senses from the objects of sense, then is his understanding well-poised."

"19. Even here on earth everything is overcome by those of balanced constant mind; Brahma is all purity and all harmony; therefore they are established in Brahma."

यः सर्वत्रानभिस्नेहस्तत्तत्प्राप्य शुभाशुभम् ।
नाभिनन्दति न द्वेष्टि तस्य प्रज्ञा प्रतिष्ठिता ॥५७॥
यदा संहरते चायं कूर्मोऽङ्गानीव सर्वशः ।
इन्द्रियाणीन्द्रियार्थेभ्यस्तस्य प्रज्ञा प्रतिष्ठिता ॥५८॥

Geeta, Chapter 2.

"20. One should neither rejoice in obtaining what is pleasant, nor sorrow in obtaining what is unpleasant ; with Buddhi firm, unperplexed, the Brahma-knower is established in Brahma."

"18. When his subdued thought is fixed on the self, free from longing after all desirable things, then it is said, 'he is harmonised.'"

"19. As a lamp sheltered from the wind flickereth not ; such is the traditional Simile of the Yogi of subdued thought, absorbed in the Yoga of the Self."

The above being an exposition of the

इहैव तैर्जितः सर्गो येषां साम्ये स्थितं मनः ।
निर्दोषं हि समं ब्रह्म तस्माद्ब्रह्मणि ते स्थिताः ॥४९॥
न प्रहृष्येत् प्रियं प्राप्य नोद्विजेत्प्राप्य चाप्रियम् ।
स्थिरबुद्धिरसंमूढो ब्रह्मविद्ब्रह्मणि स्थितः ॥ २० ॥

Geeta, Chapter 5.

यदा विनियतं चित्तमात्मन्येवावतिष्ठते ।
निःस्पृहः सर्वकामेभ्यो युक्त इत्युच्यते तदा ॥१८॥
यथा दीपो निवातस्थो नेङ्गते सोपमा स्मृता ।
योगिनो यतचित्तस्य युञ्जतो योगमात्मनः ॥१९।

Geeta, Chapter 6.

Gnana Yoga on the one hand, the following passages explain the Karma Yoga on the other :—*

"4. Man winneth not freedom from activity by abstaining from action, nor by mere renunciation (of activity) doth he rise to perfection.

"5. Nor can anyone, even for an instant, remain actionless ; for helplessly is everyone driven to action by the energies born of Nature.

"6. Who, controlling the organs of action, sitteth dwelling in his mind on the objects of the senses, that bewildered man is called a hypocrite. But who, controlling the senses by mind, O Arjuna.

---

*न कर्मणामनारम्भान्नैष्कर्म्यं पुरुषोऽश्नुते ।
न च सन्न्यासनादेव सिद्धिं समधिगच्छति ॥ ४ ॥
न हि कश्चित् क्षणमपि जातु तिष्ठत्यकर्मकृत् ।
कार्य्यते ह्यवशः कर्म सर्वः प्रकृतिजैर्गुणैः ॥ ५ ॥
कर्मेन्द्रियाणि संयम्य य आस्ते मनसा स्मरन् ।
इन्द्रियार्थान्विमूढात्मा मिथ्याचारः स उच्यते ॥ ६ ॥

Geeta, Chapter 3.

"7. With the organs of action without attachment, performeth Yoga by action, he is worthy."

"8. Perform thou right action, for action is superior to inaction, and to the inactive, even the maintenance of the body would not be possible."

"15. Know thou from Brahma action groweth, and Brahma from the Imperishable cometh. Therefore, Brahma, the all-permeating, is ever persent in sacrifice."

"19. Therefore, without attachment, constantly perform action which is duty, for, performing action without attachment, man verily reacheth the Supreme."

यस्त्विन्द्रियाणि मनसा नियम्यारभतेऽर्ज्जुन ।
कर्मेन्द्रियैः कर्मयोगमसक्तः स विशिष्यते ॥ ७ ॥
नियतं कुरु कर्म त्वं कर्म ज्यायो ह्यकर्मणः ।
शरीरयात्रापि च ते न प्रसिद्ध्येदकर्मणः ॥ ८ ॥
कर्म्म ब्रह्मोद्भवं विद्धि ब्रह्माक्षरसमुद्भवम् ।
तस्मात्सर्वगतं ब्रह्म नित्यं यज्ञे प्रतिष्ठितम् ॥ १५ ॥
तस्मादसक्तः सततं कार्य्यं कर्म्म समाचर ।
असक्तो ह्याचरन् कर्म परमाप्नोति पूरुषः ॥ १९ ॥

Geeta, Chapter 3.

"20. Janaka and others indeed attained perfection by action ; then having an eye to the protection of the masses also, thou shouldst perform action."*

It is hardly necessary to point out that Gnana Yoga and Karma Yoga, as defined in Sri Bhagavat Geeta, do not clash with each other. Gnana Yoga purifies and concentrates thought, and thus leads to truth. Karma Yoga purifies and concentrates desires, and thus leads to disinterested perfomance of duty. Gnana is true perception as opposed to Agnana (perverse perception). So pure Karma is disinteresed performance of duty as opposed to impure Karma or Akarma, (perversion of duty). Now as truth helps duty and is not opposed to it, so Gnana Yoga helps Karma Yoga and is not opposed to it.

---

*कर्मणैव हि संसिद्धिमास्थिता जनकादयः ।
लोकसंग्रहमेवापि संपश्यन् कर्तुमर्हसि ॥ २० ॥

Geeta, Chapter 3.

Section 5.—Gnana Yoga And Karma Yoga As compared in the Geeta

In Chapter 3, Verse 3, the two Yogas are mentioned, one as belonging to those who are given to contemplation and the other to those who discipline their mind and heart.*

The following Verses, in Chapter 5, go to show, how Karma Yoga and Gnana Yoga coalesce and meet.†

"2. Renunciation and Yoga by action both lead to the highest bliss ; of the two, Yoga by action is verily better than renunciation of action."

"3. He should be known as a perpetual Sannyasi, who neither hateth nor desireth ;

---

* लोकेऽस्मिन् द्विविधा निष्ठा पुरा प्रोक्ता मयानघ ।
ज्ञानयोगेन सांख्यानां कर्मयोगेन योगिनाम् ॥ ३ ॥

† सन्यासः कर्मयोगश्च निःश्रेयसकरावुभौ ।
तयोस्तु कर्मसंन्यासात् कर्मयोगो विशिष्यते ॥ २ ॥
ज्ञेयः स नित्यसंन्यासी यो न द्वेष्टि न कांक्षति ।
निर्द्वन्द्वो हि महाबाहो सुखं बन्धात् प्रमुच्यते ॥ ३ ॥
सांख्ययोगौ पृथग्बालाः प्रवदन्ति न पण्डिताः ।
एकमप्यास्थितः सम्यगभयोर्विन्दते फलम् ॥ ४ ॥

free from the pairs of opposites, O mighty-armed, he is easily set free from bondage."

"4. Children, not sages, speak of the Sankhya and Yoga as different ; he who is duly established in one obtaineth the fruits of both."

"5, That place which is gained by the Sankhyas is reached by the Yogis also. He seeth, who seeth that the Sankhya and Yoga are one."

"6. But for one without Yoga, O mighty armed, renunciation is hard to attain to ; the Yoga-harmonised Muni swiftly goeth to Brahma."

It is hardly necessary to say that Karma Yoga, as religious exercise, is the direct effect of Bhakti. Accordingly Karma Yoga, in this sense, is synonymous with Bhakti Yoga.

Verse 19, Chapter 7, briefly puts how

यत् सांख्यैः प्राप्यते स्थानं तद्योगैरपि गम्यते ।
एकं सांख्यञ्च योगञ्च यः पश्यति स पश्यति ॥ ५ ॥
संन्यासस्तु महाबाहो दुःखमाप्तुमयोगतः ।
योगयुक्तो मुनिर्ब्रह्म न चिरेणाधिगच्छति ॥ ६ ॥

Gnana becomes identical with Bhakti, when it is properly developed to the highest point. It says, the man of spiritual knowledge, *i. e.*, the *gnani* attains to Me after diverse births, when he sees Me, *i. e.*, the Personal Loving God, in all and everything.*

In Verse 47, Chapter 6, among all Yogis the highest place is given to the Yogi, who worships God with reverence and love.†

Then again in the following Verses, in Chapter 12, worshipping with reverence and love is repeated to be the best form of Yoga, while the impersonal form of worship of God is declared to be hard and displeasing.

"Arjuna asked :—‡

"1. Those whoever earnestly fixed in Bhakti, worship Thee, and those who worship

---

* बहूनां जन्मनामन्ते ज्ञानवान् मां प्रपद्यते
वासुदेवः सर्व्वमिति स महात्मा सुदुर्लभः ॥

† योगिनामपि सर्वेषां मद्गतेनान्तरात्मना
श्रद्धावान् भजते यो मां स मे युक्ततमो मतः ४७॥

‡ एवं सततयुक्ता ये भक्तास्त्वां पर्युपासते
ये चाप्यक्षरमव्यक्तं तेषां के योगवित्तमाः ॥ १ ॥

the Supreme Being as the Impersonal, Indestructible, and the Unmanifested, which of these is the more accomplished in Yoga?"

Answer :—*

"2. Those who are earnestly attached to Me, and ever in a state of communion, worship Me, with intense reverential love, these as I take it are the best in Yoga.

"3. They who worship the Indestructible, the Invisible, the Unmanifested, Omnipresent, and Unthinkable, the Unchanging, Immutable, Eternal,

"4. Renouncing and subduing the senses, every-where with Buddhi well-balanced, in the welfare of all rejoicing, these also come unto Me.

---

* मय्यावेश्य मनो ये मां नित्ययुक्ता उपासते ।
श्रद्धया परयोपेतास्ते मे युक्ततमा मताः ॥ २ ॥
ये त्वक्षरमनिर्देश्यमव्यक्तं पर्य्युपासते ।
सर्व्वत्रगमचिन्त्यञ्च कूटस्थमचलं ध्रुवम् ॥ ३ ॥
संनियम्येन्द्रियग्रामं सर्व्वत्र समबुद्धयः ।
ते प्राप्नुवन्ति मामेव सर्व्वभूतहिते रताः ॥ ४ ॥

"5. The difficulty of those whose minds are set on the Unmanifested is greater; for the path of the Unmanifested is hard for the embodied to reach."

क्लेशोऽधिकतरस्तेषामव्यक्तासक्तचेतसाम् ।
अव्यक्ता हि गतिर्दुःखं देहवद्भिरवाप्यते ॥ ५ ॥

CHAPTER VI.

THE DARSHANAS, AS THEY BEAR UPON THE TWO REVELATIONS.

Section 1.—The Nyaya and the Vaiseshika Darshana.

THE Darshanas form an important factor in the Revelation of Rationalism. The Vedanta and the Patanjala directly deal with the subject of the Divine Being. The Naya and the Vaiseshika, though they are, on the face of them, in the nature of secular sciences, deal with their subjects in such a way as to lead to the realization of the Diety. Brahma Baibarta Purana says the following :— *

"Him whom the Nyaya calls the Inexpressible as Sankara does, the learned Vaiseshikas call the Great Originator."

The Nyaya Darshana is as explained before in fact the basis, of what in the western

---

* न्यायोऽनिर्व्वचनीयश्च यं मतं शाङ्करो वदेत् ।
नित्यं वैशेषिकास्त्वाद्यं तं वदन्ति विचक्षणाः ॥

world, is called the Natural Theology. One prominent commentator of the Nyaya Darshana sets himself to show that, the world is not the product of chance, and is not without a cause. The illustrative proposition* "the mountain is known to be in flames by the smoke issuing out of it," is well known. As a study of the creation shows it to be full of intelligence and skill, it follows from the above proposition, that the First Cause of the universe is Supremely Intelligent and Supremely Skillful.

The Vaiseshika Darshana may, in the main, be called the science of the differential or relative properties of things ; it maintains that the very atoms, which compose a thing or a class of things, have distinctive and peculiar virtues. The conception of the *Visesh* or the differential of the Vaiseshika Darshana is connected with the production of the स्वाधर्म्म्य and वैधर्म्म्य which inevitably leads to the Supreme Being, as the source of all harmony. Besides it shows that *buddhi*, the spiritual faculty of man, has an un-

---

* पर्व्वतो वह्निमान् धूमात् ॥

separable relation with God. The soul is perceived by the concentration of the mind (Manas) upon it. It says that the Soul, *i. e.*, the Supreme Soul, is perceived by the concentration of the human soul and mind.*

Thus the Vaiseshika as well as the Nyaya Darshana are parts of the Rational Revelation. But further there are proofs, in even these Darshanas showing, that their authors were earnest devotionalists. Their faith in the Vedas is absolute. The Nyaya Darshana has several *sutras*, by which objections to the Vedas are stoutly refuted. In fact, that which the Nyaya Darshana proves by deductions of reasoning, *viz.*, that the First Cause is Supremely Intelligent, the Puranas exhibit emotionally. That He is also Supremely Loving, is shown in the Puranas by allegories, parables, facts and fictions. Similarly while the Vaiseshika Darshana shows that the human soul stands in inseperable relation with the Supreme Soul, the Puranas illustrate that that relation is assuring, comforting and elevating. They

---

* आत्मन्यात्ममनसोः संयोगविशेषादात्मप्रत्यक्षम् ।

show how man finds in the Supreme Being his father and mother to infinitely higher health than a little boy can expect from his earthly father, or a baby from its earthly mother.

Apparently the Vaiseshika Darshana derives the distinguising qualities of material things, from peculiar virtues supposed to be impressed severally upon different clases of atoms. But as regards the soul of man, it places it as an independent higher entity, which derives its higher qualities of one sort or other according to the way in which it applies itself to the Supreme Soul. Evidently these qualities fix and invest man with Spritual counterparts of what constitute man's relations with the persons and things surrounding him. Thus, if a man devotes himself to God as his father or as his mother, he gets an eternal Spiritual Father, or a Spiritual Mother, in the God of his heart.

Section 2.—The Two Revelations and the Vedanta.

It has been seen before that, though the Vedanta Darshana is itself emphatically the science of spirituality, it embraces also emotionalism (Bhakti) in a striking manner. As the science of spirituality as cultivated by the Hindus, it occupies the highest place. Every syllable in each of the short *sutras*, which are stringed together most methodically, contains a mine of sense. The first *sutra* introduces the subject of the Divinity. * The second expresses that which forms the cardinal conception of the Deity in all the Upanishads; in fact that which is the universal conception of the deity among all men and races. †

"God is He from whom the universe proceeds and in whom it lives and to whom it returns."

---

* अथातोब्रह्मजिज्ञासा ।

† जन्माद्यस्य यतः ।

Then it lays down that this truth the highest of all, "is borne out by the *Sastras* (sacred scriptures), and follows from all of them read together." *

Then it goes on to show that the Vedas reveal the Deity as the Supreme Personal Being, who sees and attends, and that He is not any Impersonal Force of Nature. That He is the Supreme Will, that it is devotion to Him that saves a man, and that He is the abode of Infinitive bliss. †

Having thus shown by the texts of the Vedas that Nature is not God, further on it establishes that Nature is not an entity independent of God. In short, it establishes that Nature is God's Nature, and

---

* शास्त्रयोनित्वात् ।

तत्तु समन्वयात् ।

† ईक्षतेर्नाशब्दम् ।

गौणश्चेन्नात्मशब्दात् ।

तन्निष्ठस्य मोक्षोपदेशात् ।

आनन्दमयोऽभ्यासात् ।

the manifestation of the Supreme Will. It also says that the creation is God's sport. *

Thus it is seen that Rational Revelation, although it proceeds on the dry light of reason, approaches the Emotional Revelation which is so soothing in its character.

One may well venture to say that, the Vedanta Darshana has been subjected by its friends, the commentators, to considerable oppression. Be that as it may, the Hindu idea of Maya which has received a remarkable degree of development in connection with the Vedanta Darshana, happily serves to cut short many serious difficulties, metaphysical and moral.

In the first place it solves the metaphysical difficulty, as to how the whole nature moves, lives and has its existence in God and is, at the same time, something separate

---

* अवस्थितेरिति काशकृत्स्नः ।

प्रकृतिश्च प्रतिज्ञा दृष्टान्तानुपरोधात्

भाव चोपलब्धेः ।

लोकवत्तु लीलाकैवल्यम ।

from Him. In other words, it cuts short the question how man's free will is to be reconciled with God's absolute predisposing power. This difficulty is solved thus. Nature's separation from God is God's Maya. It is a mystery of His inscrutable Will. It is something nothing. It is something, because the Supreme Being has willed to have Nature believed as different from Him. But it is nothing, because He is the essence and the soul of Nature.

Leaving, however, the metaphysical difficulty apart, the moral difficulty is, as to why there should be evil and imperfection in the world, the Lord of which is all love and all goodness. The rationalistic side of Hinduism explains this thus. It says evil and imperfection are Maya, *i. e.*, delusion. Get over the delusion, and you get over evil. But how to get over delusion? Evil is mixed up with good. If evil be delusion, so is good also. So that the rationalists are forced to come to the conclusion that in order to get rid of evil you must get rid both of evil and good, and reduce yourself to an impersonal state.

The emotionalists, the men of Bhakti, on the other hand, say evil and imperfections are God's sports. Evil as such is not a real thing. It is only a means to good. The all-loving God has created it, so that man by getting over it, may enjoy good with relish. Thus they look upon evil as a blessing, and as a capital Lila. As soon as one comes to see evil in this light, he ceases to dread it, it becomes robbed of its poison. The man thus finds it easy to triumph over and to get rid of it.

The Srimat Bhagavata, emphatically the revealation of Bhakti, is, by some regarded, as the *Bhasya* or annotation of the Vedanta Darshana, which is emphatically the revelation of Gnana. This may seem startling. But nevertheless in one sense, it is to a great extent true. The conclusions of the Vedanta Darshana are summed up, as showing that the Supreme Being is सत्यं ज्ञानमानन्दम् Srimat Bhagavata only paraphrases this in describing God as सच्चिदानन्दविग्रहः Further the Vedanta Darshana says: "If one says that Para Brahma is also a limited Brahma because of limitations ascribed by texts, that is wrong; because such texts must be read with others which show no limitations."* Such a text is the following: "He is all action, all scent, all taste, &c."

Thus the Vedic texts, which realize God as the Supreme Personality with limitless action, limitless kama, limitless scent, etc., become emphasized. It also says, that God is either sportive like men or rests by Himself. Srimat Bhagavata's Sri Krishna is only this Supreme Personality with limitless beauty, limitless love, inimitably sportive. And this Supreme Personality is '*Sat-chit-anandam.*'

Section 3.—The two Revelations and the Sankhya Darshana.

It is believed, on good grounds that, what is called the Sankhya Darshana, is not the entire Darshana of Kapil Rishi. It would seem that the entire Kapil Darshana

---

* न स्थानतोऽपि परस्योभयलिङ्गं सर्व्वत्र हि ॥ ११ ॥
न भेदादिति चेन्न प्रत्येकमतद्वचनात् ॥ १२ ॥

contained the teachings, which Bhagavat Geeta and Srimat Bhagavata reproduce the latter under the name Sankhya Yoga. In the view of Sankhya Philosophy, taken in these great sacred authorities, in fact in all the Puranas also, it presents the beautiful and charming picture of God as the Supreme Person or Purusha standing by the side of God's Nature, the pristine and pure state of the phenomenal creation, the Yog-Maya or Adi-Prakriti. This Philosophy has developed those sweet forms of devotion which realize the Jugal Murti—the sweet dual forms of Radha-Krishna or Hara-Parvati.

But to take the Sankhya Darshana as it goes, in the form of the *sutras* by Vignana Bhikshu. In this form, it is usually taken by most commentators, as a purely secular philosophy, dealing with the subjective and objective principles of Nature. The subjective principle is the human soul ; and the objective principle is nature, not as it ought to be, but as it is, the former being called the Purusha, and the latter the Prakriti. Thus according to the *sutras* known as Sankhya *sutra*, the Purusha and Prakriti are as follows; The Purusha is the passive conscious entity, passively susceptible of feelings, of joy and sorrow, but having the power to rise superior to that which awakens its consciousness and evokes its sentiency of joy and sorrow, retaining the benefit derived from such awakening and evoking: The Prakriti is the entity which has the power of awakening the consciousness and of evoking the sentiency of the Purusha, with a proneness to lapse into grossness and evil, and to reduce the Purusha to such grossness and evil.

According to this view of the Sankhya philosophy the Purusha or the soul of man is in a very uncertain and helpless state. It is apparently at the mercy of Prakriti or of circumstances. Circumstances may completely lead it to ruin. But it is assumed that it has power of rising above them. Even according to this view of the Sankhya *sutras*, the Purusha will rise over them, if it only knows the facts constituting the relation between the soul and the nature. But evidently that would be a false hope. How can mere knowledge or Gnana of the relation between man and his sorroundings, enable him to become master over them, when he begins as a mere creature of them. Help in the form of strength must come from some quarter, but this is not indicative. Is is ventured however that from what has been shown in that II sec, that the above view of the Sankhya as it is in the extant Kapila Sutras may not be correct. The Sankhya appear at one place to have let the existence of *Ishwar* as unproved by *pratakshya-praman* (perception), and to have taken up the question again, when he concludes that the cxistence of *Ishwar* is established by such other proof as he refers to in that passage. And that Sankhya admits the Supreme Soul other than the many individualized souls, as ths *sumum-genus*, is evident from many Sutras. And manifestly he uses the word *Para* at least in certain places as indicating the Supreme Being.

Thus this philosophy shows the quarter *viz.*, *Ishwar* from which help is to come to man to convert himself from the position of a creature of circumstances, to that of a master over them.

Section 4.—The Patanjala Darshana and the Two Revelations.

THE Patanjala Darshana is the science and art of focussing or concentrating the mind. It treats of Yoga which is thus defined :—

" Yoga is the prevention of distractions of the mental faculties."

" The degree of it is marked, among other things, by concentrating one's mind upon God. "

" In Him the germ of omniscience becomes infinitely developed. "

" The syllable 'Om' serves as His name. "

" The Yogi is to repeat that syllable and realize its meaning. "*

What is the result ?

---

* योगश्चित्तवृत्तिनिरोधः ॥ १ ॥ २ ॥

ईश्वरप्रणिधानाद्वा ॥ १ ॥ २३ ॥

तत्र निरतिशयं सर्व्वज्ञबीजम् ॥ १ ॥ २५ ॥

तस्य वाचकः प्रणवः ॥ १ ॥ २७ ॥

तज्जपस्तदर्थंभावनम् ॥ १ ॥ २८ ॥

" The result is that the man then realizes the Supreme, Intelligent One and the absence of obstacles. "*

Then Patanjal Rishi defines *dharana* † as being the fixation of the mind upon a particular object, and then defines *dhyana* ‡ to mean attuning the mind to the realisation of that object.

Then in the following Sutra it is laid down that when *dhyana* is confirmed the man loses consciousness of other things and the object of *dhyana* is all that appears to him, this being the state of Samadhi. §

Thus the Yoga Shastra confirms the truth of the text of the Bhagavat Geeta.

" However men approach Me, even so do I accept them, for, the path men take from every side is Mine, O Partha. " ||

---

* ततः प्रत्यक्चेतनाधिगमोऽप्यन्तरायाभावश्च ॥१॥२९॥

† देशबन्धश्चित्तस्य धारणा ॥ ३ ॥ १ ॥

‡ तत्र प्रत्ययैकतानता ध्यानम् ॥ ३ ॥ २ ॥

§ तदेवार्थमात्रनिर्भासं स्वरूपशून्यमिव समाधिः ॥३॥३॥

|| ये यथा मां प्रपद्यन्ते तांस्तथैव भजाम्यहम् ।
मम वर्त्मानुवर्त्तन्ते मनुष्याः पार्थ सर्वशः ।

In fact, an idol or image is only a means of making *dhyana* of the spiritual in a material shape. Therefore just as *dhyana* of the Supreme Being, in a particular ideal shape, results in realization of the presence of the Supreme Being in that shape, so also, when one worships God by reducing his *dhyana* to a material shape or image, he also realizes the presence of God in it. Hence it is that what is idol worship among the Hindus, is really no worship of clay or stone, but of the Supreme Spirit through this peculiar form of *dhyana*.

The Patanjala Darshana, which may well be called an experimental science, shows the unassailable position of Emotionalism or Bhakti. It shows that man can improve himself, only by directing and concentrating his desires to and on a Personal Being, who is pure and attracting, solacing and strengthening, and at the same time absolute and all-engrossing. That this is an indispensable condition for human improvement, is proved experimentally by the Yoga Shastra.

But this condition is not supplied by the Revelation of *Gnana* (Rationalism) which reveals the God-head mainly as an impersonal and all-pervading Supreme Being.

God as personal and Attracting, is the Figure upon whom all the highest human feelings—feelings of beauty, goodness, sublimeness and wonder,—gather as unto a focus, by the process of Yoga. Yoga leads to this, and Bhakti or Emotionalism is thus the basis of Yoga as taught by Rishi Patanjala. Therefore, if the truth of the results of Yoga is established, the truth of Emotional Revelation is also established. Mention has been made of what is called *Prabritti Dharma* and the *Nibritti Dharma*. The Yoga philosophy combines and reconciles them. According to the Yoga Shastra, desires are not to be suppressed as some rationalists would rather have it, but they are to be purified and strengthened by purification. Just as the stream of blood in the human body, issuing from the heart gets vitiated, in coursing through the veins, but as it gets purified by entering the lungs, and then re-flows to do its functions properly, so the desires and affections of men, vitiated by contact with external objects, are purified by directing and concentrating them unto the Fountain of all purity whence they flow back into diverse channels of righteousness and happiness. This is the teaching of the Yoga Shastra, and as the Emotional Revelation has the same effect they confirm and support each other.

CHAPTER VII.

Section I.—The General Features of the Puranas and of Vaishnavism and Shaiva-Saktism.

THE Upanishads and the Darshanas give expression to spiritual truths in the light of Rationalism or the *Gnana Kanda.* The Puranas give expression to similar truths in the light of Emotionalism or the *Bhakti Kanda.* The former scientifically demonstrate that the Supreme Spirit is all-pervading, Omniscient and Omnipotent. The latter show how, as a matter of fact, He is realized by man as his Master or Father or Mother or Lover.

The Personal Realization of the Deity is religion proper. As the associations, local or temporary, with which this Personal Realization is associated, vary, so different sects of religion come into existence. Accordingly at one time there were five sects of the Hindu religion—all worshipping the one and the same Supreme Being under different names and with different associations—the Vaishnava, the Shaiva, the

Saura, the Ganapatya and the Sakta. Of these, the Saura and the Ganapatya hardly exist now as independent sects. The Vaishnava, the Shaiva and the Sakta are the main existing sects of Hinduism. They, again, are sub-divided into some sub-sects, according to peculiarities of doctrine and faith. The Shaiva and the Sakta tenets are sometimes amalgamated so as to form one branch, while the Vaishnava tenets stand alone as forming the other branch.

The Vaishnava portion of the Puranas deals with the *Avataras* (incarnations) of Sri Vishnu and the lives of *bhaktas* (sincere devotees) which are full of goodness, purity and of exemplary self-sacrificing acts.

As regards the portion of the Puranas devoted to Shaivaism and Saktaism, the Personal Realization of the Deity, as it is in these sacred books, is not, strictly speaking, by means of *Avataras* or Incarnations. But when God is grasped by Bhakti or Emotionalism, with a certain name given to Him, legends, expressive of his Infinite Power, and parables, to explain His Infinite Love, gather round that name. Thus Shiva and Sati are the Heroes of many a spiritual poem and spiritual drama. The Shaiva and the Sakta portion of the Puranas contains these.

The Puranas, on the whole, present the Almighty God to man in the various personal relations stated above. The highest among those relations is conceived by the Vaishnavas to be this: that God is the Fairest, Sweetest and the most charming One, whose transcendental fascinations it is impossible for humanity to resist, if it would only have a glance at Him.

Although the two main divisions of Hinduism of the present day—*Vaishnavism* and *Shaiva-Saktaism*—essentially consist of the emotional revelation, they include, in common, the elements of the rational revelation contained in the Upanishads. They differ only in their emotional aspects. The Vaishnavas grasp the deity as the Supreme Personality, standing mainly in the relation of Master, Friend or Lover to Humanity; and the Shaivas and the Saktas, as the Supreme Personality, standing chiefly in the relation of Father or Mother to Humanity.

Both realize God as the fountain of protection and of grace and as the loving One after whose image man is formed. The Vaishnavas would court him as the Bridegroom of Humanity,—*Vasudeva* or Shri Krishna—the maker as well as the son of man. They find Him as such by *sadhana* or emotionalism.

The Saktas see in the Deity all the wonders of this phenomenal world, and call Her the mother though presenting Herself as the daughter of man. All this they realise by *sadhana* or emotionalism. These Divine Figures, as seen by the votary, transcend all limits of excellence, by the grandeur of thought which Rationalism supplies as the back ground of emotionalism and which transfuses the limitless into the limited. In fact, the development of Rationalism prepares the ground for the revelation of bhakti in two ways,—one is the reaction from the gradually increasing blankness and weariness which mark its progress, until it simply makes such blankness and weariness unbearable; and the other is by demonstrating that God is not only Infinite Power and

Limitless Intelligence, but verily an Ocean of Love.

Sankara Acharya, the prophet of Rationalism, himself in his later years, could not help being over-mastered by *bhakti*, as his ardent prayers to the Mother of the Universe shows. So it is said of Vyasa Deva of old, that in the first part of his life, he was the medium of that dry Rational Revelation—*the Vedanta* ;—but in the latter part of his life, that profoundest Emotional Revelation, the *Srimat Bhagavata*, came through him.

Men, for the pratical purposes of their existence, need to *get* God and not merely *to have a knowledge* of Him. One may have some impression of God without being affected by that impression. The test of getting Him, is to see whether the impression of God moves and melts the heart and moulds the life. Thus when one feels 'I have got Him,' he bursts into tears of joy. It is in the state of emotionalism or *Bhakti* alone that one gets Him. Thus it is, that those that begin in *Gnana* and in *Bhakti*

Section 2.—The Two Main Forms of Sadhana.

WORSHIP and prayer (*Sadhana* and *Upashana*) are in the main of two kinds—*niskama* (disinterested) and *shakama* (selfish). The former may be called the *sattwika*, and ths latter, the *rajasika*. Emotionalism is the basis of both. But sattwika emotionalism is purifing, elevating and enduring. The rajasika emotionalism tends to grossness and has a suicidal tendency. The *niskama* Vishnu Bhakti such as Pralhada or Dhruba possessed, not only blesses the possessor of it, but all around. But the *shakama* bhakti of Ravana to Mahadeva, although it had raised him to eminence, did not save him from destruction.

The tender love of the *Vaishnavas* for God as the all-attracting loving One, is free from selfish taint, though perhaps sometimes a little too romantic in character. The love of the Sakta for Mother Durga involves more or less of that selfishness in which a child freely indulges in teasing his mother to sastisfy his hunger and other wants. If the sefishness of the *Sakta* devotee stopped here, that would be harmless and natural. Sometimes, however, it goes beyond that, and leads his prayers in a direction of mischievousness. It is not proper, however, to institute any comparison between the Sadhana of the two sects ; for, the character of the prayer depends upon the progress of individual rather than upon the sect to which he belongs.

One important point of difference between the unselfish form and the selfish form of prayer and worship, is this. When one prays selfishly, he may get the fruits of his prayers, but they bring little peace to his mind. The Hindu Philosophy has conclusively proved it that the result of the *Raja-guna* is misery, and that a selfish course of action must lead in the direction of unrest. Hence it is that some leaders of those sects in which *sakama sadhana* (selfish prayer) prevails, are more or less driven to take shelter to that blank conclusion of Rationalism called *Nirvan Mukti* (merger in the Infinite One).

But those who pursue the modes of disinterested prayer and cultivate Sattwika Bhakti, find themselves progressing in the path of purity and bliss, and God appears to them every day the more beautiful and the more loving. They see no reason to get anxious to get rid of their personality, finding an infinite road of progress ever before them. What it is necessary to lose, is not personality, but selfish or *Rajasik* personality.

Even those who preach the necessity of losing personality, as some Adwaitabadee *Acharyas* do, cannot altogether abolish all distinction between the creation and the Lord of the creation. They distinguish the creation from the Creator, calling the former the *Maya* of the latter, thus bringing in an element of *Dwaitism*. But it is all the same a distinction. The *Adwaitabadees* explain their philosophy thus :*

"Existence, illumination, loveliness, form and name are the five things. Of these the first three constitute the form of God, the latter two of the world." So they are bound

---

* अस्ति भाति प्रियं रूपं नाम चेत्यर्थपञ्चकम् ।
आद्यत्रयं ब्रह्मरूपं जगद्रूपं ततोद्वयम् ॥

to make a distinction between the world and the Originator of the world. Man as belonging to the world, has form and name. God is the cause of man's existence, illumination and loveliness. From Him he must derive them and grow in respect of them. But how is he to develop himself in existence, illumination and loveliness? Awdaitabadees say by *Sravana*, *Manana*, and *Nididhyasana*, *i. e.*, by receiving instructions, by cogitation and by contemplation. Surely, cogitation, and contemplation come very near to devotion and prayer, which is all that *Bhakti* or emotionalism means, and which shows the futility of preaching the destruction of one's personality altogether.

Section 3.—Instances of Rationalistic and Emotionalistic Prayer or Hymn.

All prayers or hymns are more or ess emotional. But they are capable of being divided into the rationalistic and the emotionalistic. In rationalistic prayers, God is invoked more in His relation to the universe than to the individual man. Such prayers are, in short, more the dictates of reason than of love. The following prayer from the *Mahanirvana Tantra* is an instance of rationalistic prayer :

"Om, adoration to Thee, the Being of beings, the Support of the universe ;

"Adoration to Thee—the veritable conscious One, the Soul of the universe ;

"Adoration to Thee, known as the One Truth, the Giver of salvation ;

"Adoration to Thee, pervading the universe and free from qualitative defects ;

"Thou art alone to be borne in mind ;

'Thou art alone to be welcomed to the heart ;

"Thou art the Cause of this universe ;

"Thou art Universe-like in form ;

"Thou art the Lord, the Protector and the Destroyer ;
"Thou art the Supreme, the unshifting and the Perfect.
"Fear to fear itself, Dread to the dreadful ;
"The Destiny of living beings, the Purifier of the pure ;
"Thou art the Disposer of the highest position.
"The Higher than the high, the Protector of the protector ;
'The Lord above all—the Manifester of all forms ;
"The Mysterious, the True transcending all sense ;
"The Incomprehensible, the Imperishable and Inexpressible Reality ;
"The Maker of phenomena—the Protector from fall ;
"Thee alone we adore, Thee alone we meditate on ;
"Thee that bearest witness to the universe we bow to ;
"Thee the one Truth, the containing Lord and not contained ;

"The vessel to ferry over the ocean of the world, we seek protection of.

Emotionalistic prayers or hymns are uttered, invoking God, more in relation to the individual, than to the universe, and they are more dictated by love than by dry reason. The following passages from *Srimat Bhagavata* illustrate such emotional utterances. They are what may be called the hymns of the *Gopikas*.

But who are these Gopikas in the first place ? Srimat Bhagavata explains this in Sloka 27, Chapter 29, Kanda 10. The Gopikas were those who had eschewed all wordly passions for the sake of *Sri Krishna* the Supreme Lover, for whom their love knew no bounds.*

These Gopikas were enjoying the company of the Supreme Lover of all, in the most delightful Brinda-garden, full of flowering plants and beautiful trees, the birds singing on the branches, which were waving in the gentle breeze of autumn, and

---

* प्रेष्ठं प्रियेतरमिव प्रतिभाषमाणं ।
तासां तदर्थविनिवर्त्तितसर्व्व कामाः ॥

the full moon outpouring its silvery lustre over trees, plants and all. Suddenly Sri Krishna's presence they missed, and they were sunk in distress. The following verses of *Srimat Bhagavata Rasha-panchadhyaya*, Chapter 30, embody what the *Gopikas* did and said in quest of the Loving One.

"4. The *Gopikas* who, in the midst of the exquisite happiness, felt in realizing the presence of the sweet all-attracting Lord of the world, in that happy spot and at that happy hour, suddenly missed His presence, assembled together and began to sing His praise in chorus, and iike persons Who had lost their mind, began a course of search after that Wonderful Person who is inside and outside all this visible universe, by questioning every plant, tree and shrub regarding Him.

"5. Ye *Aswatha* and other monarchs of the forest, you from your tallness must have surely seen that Son of Bliss Who, having enraptured our souls with His loving smiles, in this paradise on earth, has left us alone.

"6. Ye *Asoka* and other lesser members of this forest, who bear charming and blooming flowers, to bear witness to that enticing smile of His, by which He taunts the pride of the fairest ones of this earth, ye must have seen him passing by this place.

"7. Thou *Tulasi,* so good, so fond of the lotus-feet of Hari which attracts thee as doth lotus the bee, thou must have seen that sweet Lord of thine.

"8. Ye *Malati* and ye all of the same sisterhood of sweet-scented flower-bearing plants, ye must have felt the touch of His sweet-scented hands.

"9. Ye jack tree, mangoe tree and rest of the class—ye are born to serve others with pleasure; surely you will tell us which way the all-serving One has gone, for without Him we are lost even to ourselves.

"10. Thou earth! surely thou hast undergone the best of *tapas* (penance), for thou art bristling with delight excited by the touch of His blessed feet—tell us whether or not this joy of thine is not inspired by His sweet embrace rather than the impetus of His boar-like might.

"11. Thou fair sister Gazelle! (of rolling eye and full of fragrance in the navel), did Madhava with His most beloved One, the fairest of His creation, approach thee to gratify thy longing and restless eyes. Surely the sweet scent that is here about thee, must be of that exquisite fragrance, issuing from the charming garland of His neck, which touches the breast of His most beloved One.

"12. Ye trees with bending boughs! did our beloved Lord receive your greeting with His loving look while wandering here, sporting with the fairest of His nature, followed by swarms of bees (that would hum on your buds as on the *Tulasi* leaves).

"13. Let us ask these creepers. Lo! though they are embracing the trees, it is their leaves bearing the nice tracings and colourings of our beloved Hari's hand, which make their real glory and exultation.

Section 4.—The Religion Manifested in Sri Gouranga of Nuddea.

THE sectarian spirit between sect and sect among the Hindus, should have vanished in the religion manifested in Sri Gouranga of Nuddea. That religion consists of two strata—a basical strata of universal religion, and another of a more finely developed spiritualism. The former contains the principle of earnest devotion to the Supreme Personality (Hari) and is free from any dogma or ritualism and only enjoins the chanting of God's name with all the earnestness of heart. The latter consists of the realization of love towards God, beginning from the ordinary degree of it rising to the highest.

This lofty stage of religious development is not within the scope of this little book. But all sects of Hinduism can stand embracing each other, on the basical platform of Sri Gouranga's religion—that enjoining only earnest devotion and *Nama Sankirtan.* Sri Gouranga expressly taught, that if every one proved true to his own faith, he would be saved. He, the *Avatar* of Sri Krishna, himself on one occasion, got converted into mother Durga and suckled all his followers as a mother does her children. Then, on various other occasions, he danced in ecstacy before the image of Mahadeva. This is sufficient to show the catholicity of Sri Gouranga's religion.

His religion is complete in every respect. Low intellectualism tending to supersede religion, is always to be condemned, just as idle sentimentalism tending to undermine religion. But if, beyond that, any *Vaishnava* means to condemn purified reason, then he would sin against Sri Gouranga. For the *Maha-prabhu* of Nuddea, by accepting *Sannyas*, paid that homage to *gnana* which is its best and highest demand. Besides the manner and circumstances of the conversion of *Sarbabhauma*, the prince of Rationalism, and of *Prakashananda*, the leader of Vendantists, prove that Sri Gouranga's *Krishna-Prema* is not antagonistic to Vedantaism or Rationalism, but is the goal and end of it. Thus Sri Gouranga's religion is reason tested and not opposed to reason.

As regards morality, the religion of Sri-Gouranga places it on the highest and the safest basis. He did not promulgate any moral commandments to his followers. He did not enter into detailed moral precepts as some prophets did. He simply taught: 1st That God is to be worshipped by chanting His name; 2nd That his is only the true worship who is strong like the tree, but who is at the same time bending like the grass, and who would not do homage to himself but to others.*

To transfer the figure to the animal kingdom, the expression "who is strong, like the tree" is equivalent to who has the courage of a lion, and the expression "who is bending like the grass" is equivalent to who has the meekness of a lamb. In fact, the sloka alluded to enjoins three following principles:

I. Let not adversity and temptations bend yourself.

---

* तृणादपि सुनीचेन तरोरिव सहिष्णुना।
अमानिना मानदेन कीर्त्तनीयः सदा हरिः॥

II. Divest yourself of stiffening pride and hardening selfishness.

III. Do not seek your own glory, but the glory of your fellow brothers.

It needs hardly to be explained that all rules of moral conduct are condensed in these three precepts.

These three principles of morality and spirituality are at every step exemplified in the life of Sri Gouranga.

Thus one feels not the least hesitation in calling the religion of Sri Gouranga as complete in every respect.*

* A full view of Sri Gouranga's religion is to be found in that earnest and devotional work on the subject, both in Bengali and English, by Babu Shishir Kumar Ghose.

CHAPTER IX.

MISCELLANEOUS.

Section 1.—Karma or Prarabdha.

MAN is either a creature of circumstances or a master of them.

He is a creature of circumstances, first when he is a slave to his passions ; secondly, when he is acted on, by accidental circumstances. This second case may be disregarded. Thus for all practical purposes he is a creature of circumstances when he is a slave to his passions and desires,

He is a master of circumstances when his desires are under his control.

In the *Kathopanishad* of the Black Yajur Veda, it is explained that,

"Men are influenced by either a sense of duty, or a sense of selfish attachment. The wise by a thorough judgment separate the two. The wise prefer duty to interest."

Now to follow what is *priya* or matter of selfish interest or attachment, brings on a train of consequences. When the object of a passion is half fulfilled, the passion grows stronger and tends to further action. If the man dies when thus circumstanced, such further action and its consequences transpire in the succeeding state of his existence.

This occurs not only with regard to pursuing what is *priya,* in preference to what is *sreya*, but also in pursuing what is *sreya*, or duty, if the sense of duty is mixed with selfishness. This is the law of *Karma*.

Rationalism seeks to cure it, but how ? It suggests that to get rid of *Karma-bandha*, it is neccessary to have *Gnana* or *Viveka*, *i. e.* a consciousness of the self being distinct from the objects of passions or desires. It says that when this consciousness is attained, self becomes disassociated from the objects of sense, and rises superior to them.

But however self may rise superior to objects of sense, it cannot absolutely get rid of *rajasika* attachment. By distinguishing one's soul from the object of sense, one may secure more pleasure than pain. But the utter extinction of pain is not obtained till utter annihilation of all desires. This is the conclusion of Rationalism.

But Emotionalism or *Bhakti Kanda* prevents such a despairing solution. It points out that a man may pursue desires and yet he may be saved from *Karma-bandha*, provided he surrenders himself to the Supreme Will. By such a surrender he may be saved without the necessity of annihilation; he continues a man devoted unconditionally and solely to the service of the Supreme Lord of his heart.

Bhagabat Geeta has explained this most forcibly and most clearly. It is not necessary to dwell on this subject at length in this little book. It is sufficient to say that what is a burden according to Rationalism is a privilege according to Emotionalism. For if man had not the liability and the benefit of his actions, nothing to call his own, and would have thus nothing to offer to his God as grateful presents and nothing to invoke His aid to save himself from. It is the law of *Karma* that enables man to offer his good belongings to God as presents of love, and his bad belongings as expiatory presents to be saved from them.

The bond of *Karma*, as it operates with

regard to acts of a previous birth, has not, strictly speaking, any moral aspect ; for, the man does not remember what he did before. But the forgetfulness engendered by a new birth, proves only the goodness of the Divine Law, which, by causing the rebirth, removes the acuteness of suffering, arising from consciousness of a bad course of past life, and at the same time leaves the man free to get rid of the suffering altogether by absolute faith in the Lord of his existence, who knows how to weld the consequences of one's past *Karma*, into His universal loving design.

Section 2.—The Future State of Man.

THE doctrine of transmigration of soul is a well-known doctrine of Hinduism. It is the counterpart of the doctrine of *Karma.* But, as with regard to *Karma*, so with regard to the doctrine of transmigration of soul, Rationalism and Emotionalism differ in their views. Rationalism driven by its logic to a perpetual train of *Karma-bandha* till *Nirvan* or extinction, sees in transmigration of soul an inflexible fatality by which each man must incessantly go up and come down, now going into a higher body and now into a lower.

But Emotionalism or *Bhakti* experiences the consoling truth that, so long as a man gives up himself disinterestedly to good work, by devoting himself to do the will of the Supreme Lord, he only goes higher and higher up, putting on progressively finer and finer bodies, thus approaching the feet of the Lord of his existence.

To *Bhakti Kanda* transmigration is a punishment designed for the hopelessly retrograde few for whom compulsion to assume grosser bodies owing to sin and vice may be a success of redemption. The idea of transmigration of soul, thus, serves as the idea of hell to deter one from weaked pursuits. When a man wants to rise to a higher stage of existence, without deserving it, he finds himself hurled back. But when he makes earnest efforts to rise and gradually makes himself worthy of rising, he remains in one or other of the finer bodies—the astral body and the like, and finds himself in better company and nearer the ultimate and the highest paradise, in which the loving presence of the Supreme Lover of beings is incessantly felt and realized. *Gnana Kanda* or Rationalism is always apt to concern itself with the question—what will become of man when all progress is ended. It says, then man must begin again. It may be so. But this is too remote a question to require any practical consideration. The immediate question is, does man exist after death? He does exist, according to both the Revelation of *Gnana* and the Revelation of *Sadhana*. In this mortal body man cannot enjoy out all that he deserves to enjoy, nor suffer all that he deserves to suffer. In the next world he continues to enjoy and suffer. According to the common belief, the state of enjoyment is called heaven, and the state of suffering is called hell. The state immediately next after death must be more or less temporary. After that state he must either rise or fall. When he rises, he assumes a finer body. When he falls, he reverts to his former human birth or perhaps goes even lower than that. In the temporary unsettled state after death, the man is in need of help, just as the new-born child on earth is. He gets this help from those departed friends and relations who may be in the next world. The Hindu *Shastras* provide also for help to be rendered by relations left on this earth, by prayer and devotion in the shape of what is called *sradha*. In short, Rationalism looks upon transmigration indiscriminately as a law of fatality and compulsion, whereas Emotionalism looks upon it as a law which imposes fatality and compulsion on those who have sinned and erred, but which leaves a free choice to those who have lived well. These latter may come down if they like; but they may also elect to remain in the higher spheres in the company of their departed friends and relatives who may be living in those spheres.

Section 3.—The open names of the Deity.

THE names of the Deity in the Hindu religion naturally range themselves either on the side of one or other of the two Revelations of *Gnana* and *Bhakti* or *Sadhana*. *Para-Brahma* and *Parama-Atma* are names on the side of the *Gnana Kanda*. The names,—Sri Vishnu, Sri Bhagwan, Sri Hari, Siva,—on the other hand, are on the side of *Bhakti*. The names of the *Gnana Kanda* generally imply intellectual conceptions, such as Infinity, Omnipotency, etc. The names of the *Bhakti Kanda*, on the other hand, carry with them various sweet and lovely associations, moral and historical.

There is a third class of names which are rather of a colourless character, combining the essential import of both the other two classes. These names are such as *Parama-Ishwar*, *Param-Devata, etc.* These names correspond to the name God in the European languages. The European languages are branches of the same family of languages as the Sanskrit and other Indian languages. The important words in all the Indo-European languages have a common root, such as father, mother, brother, etc. How is it. then, that as regards this most important name—the name of the Supreme Being,—this European name 'God' is different from the Indian names? The following observations will show that it is not different. The name God appears to have travelled into the West in a somewhat unusual way from the East. In the Vedas we fiud *Daksha* as being the Supreme Lord of the creation—the *Projapati.* He is conceived as being wedded to *Aditi* or Infinity, and He produced all things and beings, as conceived in the womb of Infinity. Now it is seen that, in many words, the letters are reversed, in course of their transit from the mouth of the men of a certain class or of a certain locality, to the mouths of another class or loeality. Various instances of this, may be given. What is *sukha* (happiness or pleasure) in the Indian languages is *khush* in the languages on the west of the Indus. If we descend to colloquial expressions, the instances of such reversal of letters are numerous. So it seems *Daksha* became *Khoda* on the other side of the Indus. Then *Khoda* became *Goda* in middle Europe (Germany). The *Goda* became God in the further west. The name *Daksha* came to be an equivalent of *Parama Ishwara* in Europe, while in India it degenerated into a *Pauranik* sense. Regarding the name, God, we find the following in Webster's Dictionary : "As this word and *good* are written exactly alike in Anglo-Saxon, it has been inferred that *God* Was named from his *goodness.*"—But the corresponding words in most of the other languages are not the same; and it is believed, no instance can be found of a name given to the Supreme Being from the attribute of goodness. It is probably an idea, too remote from the rude conceptions of men in early ages. With the exception of the word *Tehoua,* the name of the Supreme Being appears usually to have reference to his supremacy or power, and to be equivalent to lord or ruler. In the present case, there is some evidence that this is the sense of this word; for in Persian, *Gods* or *Khoda,* signifies lord, master, prince or ruler.

Section 4.—The Secret Names of the Deity.

It has been already shown that, ceremonies are helps to *Sadhana* and *Karma Kanda*. Some ceremonies, such as sacrifice or worship, are in general openly celebrated. But there are other ceremonies which are required to be performed in secret. In fact, secrecy is an exceedingly useful means of securing gravity and seriousness. The worship and prayer of the Hindu Religion is accordingly of a two-fold form. The one consists of ceremonies in public; the other is performed in secret, in the recesses of one's heart. The former is occasional. The latter is enjoined daily and is called the *Ahnika*.

The daily prayer of the Hindu is conducted as a matter of the utmost individual importance. It is as necessary as the daily food. This prayer is essentially secret. The *Guru* initiates him in it. He adopts a name for the Deity, which is unknown to others. It is some syllable which has an elastic meaning. The meaning of the syllable is widened and deepened, as the man grows in spirituality and piety. Among the worldly relations of man that which forms the keystone of a his happiness—the conjugal relation—owes its depth and sacredness largely to the secret character of its intimacy. Likewise, the highest of a man's spiritual relations—that with the Lord of his soul, is sweetened and deepened by cultivating it in secrecy, away from this public gaze. The *diksha mantra* is a secret, as are the *mantras* of such Societies as the Masonic or the like. It forms, in short, an occultism.

The efficacy of the *ahnika* or daily prayer as described above, is, indeed, great. The daily prayer, if earnestly carried on, puts the man in the way of acquiring spirituality daily and of advancing in communion with God. It is, no doubt, in one sense artistic. But as already observed, the *Karma Kanda* it-self is wholly like an art. It is an art which focuses the radiating spirituality of the Great Spiritual sun of the physical universe. As you can focus the rays of the physcial sun and cause it to burn, so by *bhakti* you may focus the spiritual halo of Sri Vishnu or Sri Krishna. The mystic name given to Him, consisting of a particular syllable, daily gains in meaning and force, so as to draw closer and closer the thread of communion between the votary and the God of his heart.

Such is the great importance of the system of secret individual prayer which the Hindu Religion enjoins, side by side with the external ceremonies and forms. This system of prayer as embodied in *Karma Kanda* or Emotionalism, is evidently not inconsistent with the *jnana Kanda* or Rationlism.

This little book, the aim of which is to give a general idea of the Revelation of Rationalism and of the Revelation of Emotionalism, and to point out that the one is like a science, and the other like an art, may well be concluded by saying that the formula, एकमेवाहितोयम्, [The one without a second.] shortly expresses the essence of the Revelation of Rationalism, and the song, देहि देहि चरणमधुपानम् [let me drink a drop of the nectar of thy feet] expresses the essence of the Revelation of Emotionalism.

THE END